March 24, 1998

Daughters Of Dakota

Stories from the Black Hills

edited by
Sally Roesch Wagner

Volume 6

GFWC of SD/DOD
Box 349
Yankton, SD 57078

*To Angie,
My Best Wishes,
Sally Roesch Wagner*

Copyright © 1994 by Sally Roesch Wagner.
All rights reserved. Printed in the United States.

ISBN 1-880589-06-0 (Volume 6)
ISBN 1-880589-00-1 (Set)

Cover photographs are from the Centennial Archives, Deadwood Public Library. All other photographs are from the Pioneer Daughters collection of the General Federation of Women's Clubs of South Dakota. The collection is housed in the South Dakota Historical Society.

DAUGHTERS OF DAKOTA
Box 349
Yankton, SD 57078

To Clara Lobdell
who
first schooled me on Black Hills women
and
taught me
there ain't nothin' a woman can't fix
with a hairpin, a touch of ingenuity, and a healthy helping of
elbow grease

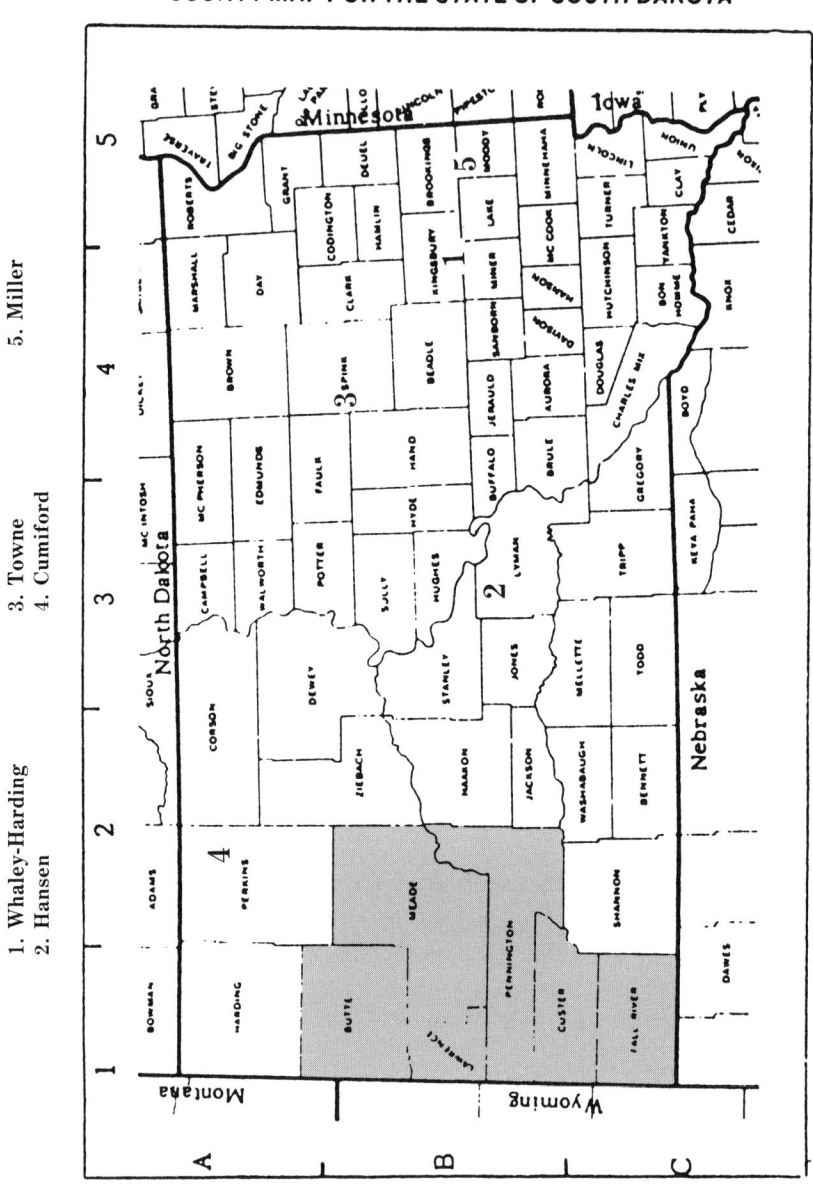

TABLE OF CONTENTS

County Map ---- iv
Acknowledgments ---- vii
Introduction ---- ix

THE EXPERIENCE
  History of Thomas H. Russell Family ---- 1
  The Trip Here ---- 5
  Women Homesteading on their Own ---- 24
  Once Here ---- 30
  The Wild West ---- 39
  Food ---- 45
  Water ---- 50
  Indians ---- 54
  Travel ---- 64
  Adversity and Overcoming ---- 68
  Blizzards, Cyclones and Fires ---- 73
  Social Life ---- 76
  Marriage ---- 82

THE WOMEN
  Catherine Maud Boland Arbuckle ---- 86
  Ellen Boyce Bryant ---- 91
  Armilda Matherly Gamet Cole ---- 96
  Annie Rozenkranz Fish ---- 100
  Laura Belle Gamut ---- 105
  Mattie Curtis Jennings ---- 114
  Clarabelle Liggett Pouriea ---- 120

Mariah Jane Williams Ford --------------------------------- 120

Christina Anderson Frawley -------------------------------- 122

Alvina Schleichardt Parsons ------------------------------- 125

Jessie Gannon Handlin Keene ----------------------------- 128

Della A. Michaels -- 129

Minnie Petersen Meier -------------------------------------- 133

Amelia J. Miller --- 138

Mary Doody Mochon -- 142

Minerva Ellen Morris and Minnie Williamson ------------ 147

Maude D. Ogden -- 149

May Edna Painter --- 152

Alice Dinnis Ham -- 156

Mae Florence Spruling Letteer Hudson ----------------- 157

Ella Teed Richards --- 160

Ella Grant Ames Vallery ----------------------------------- 164

Lucy Volland --- 166

Acknowledgments

Dawn Schatz organized the data entry and the logistics of the book. LaVera Rose fact-checked, tracked-down contextual information, located the photos, and told great jokes. Ellie Potts gave me a boost of encouragement. Terri Davis of the Deadwood Public Library kept herd on the cover photos, and saw to it that I got them.

You, the readers of the series keep me going with your enthusiasm. Please send me your comments and suggestions.

Poem

Written by the sister of one of the women in the Pioneer Daughters collection, this poem sets the stage for the stories to come.

> I sit and dream, as old folks do,
> Of all the vanished years.
> Now I am old and of the past
> but still, I played my part.
>
> I made new paths for tired feet,
> gave many a man a start.
> Old actors are forgotten
> upon the world's great stage.
>
> A few scant lines for <u>Pioneers</u>
> upon the printed page,
> who toiled and suffered,
> knew not ease, and little asked of fate.
>
> Old men and women in the sun,
> so near the close of day,
> wonder if you remember
> as you pass along the way. 1

Here is the remembering.

Introduction

There is no story of the Black Hills; there are at least four, as Indians and non-Indians, men and women, experienced the region, lived its history, in qualitatively different ways. This book represents a part of a part of the Black Hills story. There are no stories of Lakota women. Their stories must be told separately, and in their own book. The rich and extensive Pioneer Daughters Collection of stories (gathered by the General Federation of Women's Clubs of South Dakota), which have been edited here, represent the "good girls" of the Hills; the prostitute's stories never found their way into the collection. There are also notable absences of important women in the region during this time period, such as the author Estelline Bennett. They don't appear, simply because their stories are not contained in the Pioneer Daughters collection.

Also absent are the first two non-Indian women who came into the Black Hills. The story of the first, the African-American cook on Custer's 1874 expedition into the Hills, Sarah Campbell, is contained in volume one of the Daughters of Dakota series. The first white woman to enter the Black Hills, Annie D. Tallent, requires a book to herself, as the schools in the state move to disassociate themselves from this viciously prejudiced woman. Her history, and the history of the removal of her name from educational honors, is the subject of a booklet by the author entitled, "Annie D. Tallent, Goodbye Forever: A People Rename Themselves" (Sky Carrier Press, 1994). The Black Hills stories contained so many anecdotes about teaching, careers, medical care, and birthing that a separate book will be done on these topics.

Today we know the disrespect and contempt contained in the word "squaw"; had these pioneer women known what we know, they would undoubtedly not have used the word. In respect to them and their Native American friends, I have changed that word whenever it has appeared in the manuscript, along with the words "papoose" and "buck".

"Colored" and "Negro" are no longer considered correct usage; African-American has replaced them in the women's stories.

Endnotes will help you track-down the stories you want to know more about. Editing has been light, simply honing the original manuscripts, with an attempt to maintain regional language and grammatical rules (which bear little resemblance to King's English).

Before charges of favoritism emerge, let me hasten to assure you that the greater frequency of Lawrence County stories does not reflect a particularly soft spot in the editor's heart for Deadwood and Lead (although she has one), but rather, the greater number of stories from that county in the Pioneer Daughters collection.

History of Thomas H. Russell Family
by Laura Russell Sentman, daughter
Lawrence County
1878

"On April 6, 1875, they were taken out by the militia to Fort Laramie, discharged from the Fort and told to stay out of the Black Hills as it was Indian Territory and not open to settlement. In 1876, it was opened for settlement." The history of the white settlement of the Black Hills is contained in the interval between these two sentences from this story, told by the daughter of one of the first whites to come into the Hills with the intention of staying.

Father was connected with the Sioux City Times. Charley Collins was owner of the Times. In 1874, Mr. Collins and my father organized the Collins-Russell Expedition (sometimes referred to as the Gordon Party). The expedition was composed of twenty-six men, one woman and a boy. I do not have to go into detail about the trip to the Black Hills as it is all written up in "The Black Hills or Last Hunting Ground of the Dakotahs" by Annie D. Tallent, who, with her husband and nine-year-old son, was a member of the party.

They left Sioux City October 6, 1874, six outfits in all. They called their covered wagons, which were drawn by two pair of oxen, "outfits." There were also five saddle horses and two greyhounds, "Dan and Fan." They became pets of the entire party, and a donkey they called "Jack", that they picked up on the way, also afforded lots of amusement and trouble.

After traveling seventy-eight days enroute, they arrived at their destination, about two-and-a-half miles below Custer, and built the Custer Stockade in December, 1874, where they spent the winter. On April 6, 1875, they were taken out by the militia to Fort Laramie, discharged from the Fort and told to stay out of the Black Hills, as it was Indian Territory and not open to settlement.

In 1876, it was opened for settlement.

Father returned in 1877 as Agent for the Union Pacific Railroad in Deadwood. The coach line connected with the Union Pacific at Sidney, Nebraska. The stagecoach and U.P. Office was located on Main Street. Father remained as Agent of the

U.P.R.R. until the Northwestern built into Rapid City. He would not take a transfer as he preferred to remain in the Hills.

He bought three lots on Centennial Avenue when the town was laid out and built a home for us. Our house was finished in April, 1878 and he sent for mother, brother Percy and myself. Father met us at the coach station on this side of the Cheyenne River, which mother said was a raging torrent. We had to cross in a rowboat. She put her hand on the side of the boat and her fingers touched water. She said she never knew how she lived through it, until they reached the other side. The day before we crossed, one of the boats tipped over and two people were drowned.

After the coach had changed horses and we got something to eat, we were on our way to the Black Hills. Just imagine mother with two babies and a African-American girl whom she brought with her. It took three days and two nights on the way. There were several other ladies with small children and babies who came under similar conditions; Mrs. Bullock, Mrs. Wringrose, Mrs. Hunter, Mrs. Merrick and others.

When the coach, driven by six horses, made the turn up Deadwood's Main Street, the driver snapped his whip and the horses galloped up Main Street to the office to unload. It was quite an event to go downtown to see the coach come in every day.

There were four of us children. The first thing I remember was the big fire in 1879 that burned down all of Main Street, part of Sherman Street where it started, and part of Williams Street. I remember all the men in the office came up and spread wet blankets and wet bed quilts over the top of our house. Father, mother and Maggie, the African-American girl, pumped water from the cistern into wash tubs. Everyone had a cistern or well at that time.

In 1883, came the flood that wiped out the center of Deadwood. A lady living on Ingleside had a pet bird. She was caught downtown on the other side of the creek and could not get home to feed this bird, so she stood on the bank of the creek and flapped her arms, like the wings of a bird, and yelled, "Feed my bird, feed my bird." The children all took it up and played "Feed my bird", flapping their wings and yelling "Feed my bird."

Then it was time to start to school and there was no schoolhouse left to go to, as the schoolhouse and church on

Sherman Street had gone down the creek. So, one of the primary teachers started a private school in her home where we all started our first year of school. Soon after, the main building of our present school was finished. When the Sisters of the Holy Cross built St. Edward's Academy, my brother and I were sent there to school. They took boys up to fourteen years of age. Later on, about 1898, we had a Dancing School, and that is where we all learned to dance. Also a little group of High School girls organized Aurora Borealis Club. Then the Olympic Club was organized by the young men of our town and it was not long before we were all engaged to be married.

My father organized the Black Hills Pioneer Society and was the first president. I am a member of the Black Hills Pioneer Society and a former member of the Round Table Club of Deadwood. My father died in 1899 and my mother in 1915.2

Chris and Christina Callesen, who moved to the Black Hills from Yankton County in 1884. Christina rode horseback all the way across the state to her new home.

The Trip Here

Husbands came first; and illegally, the earliest ones. It was in 1876, when the men forced the hand of the United States government by refusing to obey the terms of the treaty the government had made with the Great Sioux Nation in 1868. By that Ft. Laramie Treaty, the Black Hills (along with all land west of the Missouri River to the Big Horn Mountains) would forever be the Lakota's, until the Indians agreed to change it by treaty. Ignoring the treaty, the men flocked into the Black Hills.

By the time the husbands sent for their wives and children two years later, in 1878, the government had (illegally) seized the Black Hills, and the resistance of the Lakota, who had attempted initially to drive out the settlers, was coming to an end.

The stories of the husbands of '76 are filled with that conflict between the Indians and the invaders. The stories of their later-arriving wives and children carry only the echoes of it -- the fear that never materialized.

"My uncle, E. I. Moore, willed me a farm of eighty acres which brought me to South Dakota," said Mrs. Wilson. "My husband and five children and I came by train from Indiana in 1904 and we bought an additional eighty acres to go with the farm.3

Our home was Yankton. We left late in the fall on a boat (the C.K. Peck) and went to Pierre. It was the last trip this boat or any other made that year. Consequently we were many days enroute as the water was too low in the Missouri and many sand bars were in our way. Finally, not many miles out of Pierre, they ran the boat into a very protective place as to the shore, and left it for the winter and the only passengers by that time were told we were going that evening in a wagon to an Indian Camp to stay the night and to breakfast. Then we would be taken on to Pierre in the morning, which was done. The quarters in the Camp were immaculately clean with a fine bed for us in white sheets, etc., and their meals were good.

From Pierre we came by stagecoach, but we missed the first coach so left the next day for Rapid City. My mother was

decidedly against coming any farther west to live than Yankton and most fearful of the Indians and highwaymen.
     That night about twelve o'clock our coach was stopped. Mother thought, of course, that highwaymen were holding up the coach, a thing that often happened. And I can remember how she was shaking when she finally wakened me, and she was holding me on her lap, when a man from the other coach called out, "Any women aboard?" And our driver of the six horses said, "Yes, a woman and child." Then father said, "That is them" and came over to the coach and rode back with us. 4

     Mrs. Orpha Haxby, who had come with her people the year before, was one of the children on hand who watched the twelve-year-old Martha Lewis step from the wagon, dressed in her best, complete with small parasol. A friendship of long years' standing started there, and Martha admitted many years later that had the train not stopped outside of the settlement a short time before, to give the women time to array themselves in their best, the entree might not have been so grand. The Lewis family liked the looks of the country, and Mother Lewis was weary of wandering. Although William had been quite successful in his various locations, he was a wanderer, ever looking for new horizons. Mary Lewis said, "We have had enough of wandering. We have lost enough in the burying of our babies, and in looking for new lands. Here we stay," and stay they did.5

     Driving eight milk cows -- four yoke -- hitched to a wagon laden with 4,000 pounds of groceries, he braved the trip overland through the Indian country and entered the enchanted Hills via Buffalo Gap. He was accompanied on the perilous journey by his courageous wife, who drove a team of horses hitched to a spring wagon containing herself and four young children.
     Everly, with only seventy-five cents left at the end of the journey, was poor in worldly goods. He was rich in pluck and perseverance, however, and commenced at once to build a cabin and raise a garden. Potatoes at that time cost $15.00 a hundred weight. He saved the eyes of his potatoes and put them in sand. They not only grew but produced some of the finest potatoes he and his neighbors had ever seen. 6

I do not remember just the number of people in the party, but I do recall his telling us children about Wild Bill and Calamity Jane -- especially of Wild Bill's ability in handling a six-shooter and his skill as an Indian scout during the long journey. He said that "Calamity" drove an ox team of six or more yokes strung out on from two to four wagons and could handle them equally as well as (and many times better than) the average man. When Wild Bill was killed, my father happened to be in Deadwood that day and attended the trial of Jack McCall.

In June 1877, my father came to Cheyenne to meet mother with us six children. It was truly thrilling for the wide-eyed youngsters from the east. Every night, camp was made by drawing the wagons close in a circle which would form a sort of barricade.

One day they allowed my sister and me to ramble on ahead for we were tired of riding. We were supposed to wait at a bridge but we didn't find it for we went picking wild flowers and strayed off the trail. When we were missed they sent soldiers hunting us. They found two weary little girls sitting down to rest and wondering why the wagons hadn't come. 7

My father and mother, four brothers and I came by covered wagon over the Bismarck Trail in 1880. We had a rather good team of horses of which we were proud, "not having to use oxen". We had a good saddle horse, and a cow, and six precious hens in a box on the back of the wagon.

We traveled alone, that is without benefit of wagon train. There were several bad storms on the way, and it took us two months to make the trip.

Our parents succeeded in making us children believe it was silly to be afraid of the Indians. Later I learned they had been very worried about the Indians all the way.

My mother said, after settling in our cabin, she had difficulty getting us smaller children to sit at table and eat -- we would grab our plates and go sit on the floor, having formed the habit on our long trek from the east. 8

As my mother was coming into the Black Hills by stagecoach from Sydney, Nebraska, she and another young lady on the coach became very tired of riding, and when the coach stopped to change horses decided to walk down the road a short distance. The stage driver cautioned them about Indians, so they did not venture too far. But as they were walking along, they saw two riders on horseback coming over a little knoll. My mother and her companion ran as fast as they could back to the stagecoach and climbed inside. When the two men on horseback arrived, they proved to be two cowboys. They asked the stage driver to have the two ladies step out into the road. My mother and her companion complied. The cowboys said, "Thank you. We just wanted to see what a white woman looked like, we haven't seen one for such a long time." Mother said she and the other young lady were very content to ride in the coach the rest of the way into Deadwood.9

"I came here in a covered wagon in 1877 from Sioux City, Iowa, when I was only four-years-old," said Mrs. Blow, then she laughed and added: "It's funny the things you remember from childhood -- such as our cow, Bessie." It seems that Bessie, a cow pioneer to the hills, walked leisurely along behind the covered wagon. But you couldn't always trust Bessie, so the children followed along to see that she kept going. So, like Annie Tallent, Mrs. Blow walked part of the way from Sioux city to the Black Hills.

Bessie later came in handy as she had some seniority over the cows that went to make one of the early-day dairies in Central City which Mrs. Blow's father operated. 10

Lillian and her sister, Daisy, spent the first night in the Hills lost in the woods near Crook City. They were frightened by the bearded miners and ran into the woods and hid in a hollow log. They were found unharmed the next morning.11

"There was a lawyer in O'Neill, Nebraska, who advised us to stay away from the wild and lawless Black Hills," said Mrs. Maurice Holly. "We, that is my parents, my husband, small son, Jerry, and myself, had stopped in O'Neill. It was St. Patrick's Day, 1890, and my father went to buy a length of green ribbon for our hair." The lawyer (she never knew his name) was on his way back to Deadwood where he was to attend Federal Court. Evidently the lawyer had come up against some pretty hard cases as he had no good words for the frontier towns of the

Hills. He said that Rapid City was a little hay camp and would never amount to a hill of beans. 12

"The covered wagon moved slowly with the horses going at a walk because father and some of his friends were trailing fifty head of cattle along. The cows had to have a night watchman for safety.

Mrs. Turner recalls seeing the stagecoach come in at a terrific speed and found out it had been held up, relieved of its gold bricks, with the bandits making their escape with all the loot. The Dennis family stopped at Hill City, which was then a deserted mining camp with no one living in it except Mr. and Mrs. Trimmer and their three little girls.

"We took refuge in a cabin near the Trimmer family and Father worked in the mines for a year. It was early in 1880 when we left there, bringing with us several of Father's friends," Mrs. Turner recalls. 13

Anna came to Dakota Territory in 1881. Her father, her sister, Eva, and three brothers, came from San Antonio, Texas, by horse-drawn covered wagon. The Jackson boys drove 400 head of horses through to Custer. They had to have several riders because the horses had to be watched day and night. It took two or three months to make the trip because it was in the spring and many colts were born along the way, which delayed the travellers because they would have to wait for the colt to become strong enough to travel.

Anna and Eva Jackson enjoyed the adventurous journey. "It was a tiresome trip," she said, "but we saw lots of beautiful country and also some desert. Sometimes the rivers were up and we had to wait for the flood waters to go down before we could ford the rivers. The most troublesome part of the trip was coming through the Indian Territory. The Indians wanted some of the horses." 14

"It was the climate and mild winters that brought my folks here in 1889 when I was only three years old. We came by train from Minnesota to Buffalo Gap where uncle met us with horses and sled. My mother's parents were already here and had written about the mild climate. We located three-and-one-half miles south of Custer. The place is now known as Kingsville." 15

Triphene Marie Campion was born in Marmosa, Ontario, Canada. She came to the United States to visit her sister, Mrs. W.F. Long in the Vale community in the latter part of the last century. She never returned to Canada except for a visit several years later. She taught school in Vale and in 1898 was married to Samuel S. Littlefield, a native of Maine who had homesteaded in Whitewood Valley in the early eighties. Mr. Littlefield was elected to serve as State Representative from Meade County that year and they were married just before he was to go to Pierre so their honeymoon was spent in Pierre.16

In late spring of 1884, Chris and Christena Callesen were moving to the Black Hills. They loaded a prairie schooner with their most necessary possessions and Christena was to drive the team. Her brother and another young man wanted to go to the Hills so they rode horseback and helped Chris drive the herd of young cattle. Also accompanying the Callensens were my grandfather and his daughter, who drove her own vehicle -- a one-horse buggy. She and her nine-year-old daughter Jennie were going directly to visit her sister and family, while grandfather was going to his son, where he was to file on land adjoining.

The first day of driving the team proved too monotonous for Christena. Thereafter Grandfather Thybo drove the team. But Christena did not elect to ride in the buggy. She rode horseback all the way across the state even though her assistance was not especially needed to drive the herd of stock. Camping for meals and overnight made jobs for everyone. Days and weeks they travelled - and strangely enough this one family trekking across the state was not joined by other prairie schooners. 17

She was the mother of four children when her husband decided to go to the Black Hills to start a new life in Dakota Territory. He had heard exciting tales of the new territory from Mrs. Woods' brother-in-law, John Glover, who had been to the Hills. Glover accompanied the Woods on their journey to the Hills. Mrs. Wood's daughter, Mary, was thirteen-months-old when they started out in the wagon, trailing one horse and a mule. They traveled through Nebraska and entered the Black Hills from the south. The trip took five weeks, but Mrs. Woods said the family did not suffer any hardships enroute, although "the baby cried all the way." 18

     From Duluth, Minnesota they took a train to Bismarck, North Dakota. From there it took them three days and two nights to get to Deadwood by stagecoach. They arrived in Deadwood late in the evening after the big Deadwood fire. A friend of her husband's gave up his bed so they could get a good night's rest. The bed was just a mattress on the floor up above one of the stores. 19

    Mrs. Wringrose, her husband and small daughter sailed for the new world in the year 1875, to join her brother James Browning, and arrived in Bismarck, Dakota Territory in 1876. While in Bismarck a daughter named Ethel was born.

    When the gold rush to the Black Hills began, her brother, James Browning, decided to join the many settlers and he first set up a small grocery store in Crook City; then he decided to come to Deadwood. The Wringrose family followed her brother and arrived by coach to Deadwood in May, 1878. A partnership business was set up known as the Browning and Wringrose Grocery.20

    The father, an energetic young man, was lured to the Black Hills by the gold rush tales, coming by freight train, arriving in 1876 at Deadwood, South Dakota. One year later he returned to his former home at Blair, Nebraska, bringing his wife and year-old daughter to the Hills with him and settling in Spearfish Valley. He was a farmer and blacksmith by trade.21

    Mrs. Thompson was born in Dunserman, Scotland, and came to the United States at the age of four with her parents, Mr. and Mrs. John D. Johnstone. They lived in Pennsylvania for a short time and then moved to Iowa where they lived for six years. They lived in Wyoming and returned to Iowa before settling in Deadwood in 1879.22

On the morning of June 2, 1885, a caravan of covered wagons, consisting of eight wagons with forty-six men, women and children, left their homes on the Republican River in Nebraska to establish their own homes in Dakota, on the prairie lands, or in the valleys of the Black Hills. Andy Ball, twenty-eight, with a love for adventure combined with a desire for land of his own, with his wife and two small children joined this group. No stories are told of hardships encountered on this trek, across a thousand miles of unknown country, into a country where Indians were yet resentful over losing their land.

When the wagon train reached the Loup River after travelling several days in rain with no wood to build their campfires, they found the river out of its banks and were forced to camp for more than a week. Some of the party wished to remain there, but others, coming from Kansas, a country where wood was scarce, were anxious to go on into a timbered country. 23

We traveled in covered wagons, traveled together in a party of several families and all camped together nights. We brought horses and cattle with us, also milk cows. We crossed the river at Chamberlain on the Ferry Boat and the stock had to swim the river; we were so excited but all got across. Oh, I remember the milk cows, so we had plenty of milk, and I remember we had a barrel churn. Father had it fastened on the side of one of the wagons. They would strain the milk in that churn, and the shake of the wagon would churn and every night we would look when they opened it to see the butter. Mother was a good cook, she would bake in a Dutch oven. We also had a little sheet-iron stove. There was three of us small children.24

George T. Doud and his step-son, Tillman Payton, drove freight wagons to the Black Hills using oxen teams. They liked the Black Hills so much that they moved the family here but rented mule teams so the trip would not be so tiring. They said it cost them $35.00 to rent the mule team.25

Orpha LeGros, the youngest of a family of three daughters, was born in 1867 in Elk Point. At the age of nine years she came to Rapid City with her parents and two sisters,

Lavinia and Carrie. It took seven weeks to make the trip by ox team, including a week's delay at Pierre while the party waited for the Missouri river to freeze so that they could cross over. At that time all that identified Pierre from the rest of the vast prairies was a stagecoach stopping place.

The LeGros family traveled with a party made up of seven or eight wagons for it was unsafe to travel alone because of Indians. No encounters were experienced by the caravan but an occasional fresh grave bore mute evidence that not all who passed that way had escaped the deadly arrows.

There were only two other families, the Johnsons and Bunkers, in Rapid City when the LeGros family arrived on December 4, 1876. The entire community consisted of a few cabins on Rapid Street between fourth and fifth streets. There were no shops in which to buy gifts and no markets from which to buy food, but the women of the settlement felt that there should be a community dinner on Christmas. With their meager supplies, the preparations for that first Christmas dinner rivaled those of the Cratchit family in Dicken's Christmas Carol.26

Mrs. Jacob Lampert (nee Helena Kresse) came to Rapid City, South Dakota from Wisconsin in June, 1881. Her husband had come early in the year, and she followed; coming by train to Pierre and by stagecoach, across the state. The coach was so crowded that she had to hold the youngest of her four children on her lap, all the way.

She had been warned that there might be Indians holding up the coach, but everything was peaceful and they arrived in Rapid City after two days and nights on the road.27

The C.R. Wells family, of which Mrs. Hubbard (Jennie) was a member, came overland in a covered wagon from Pierre in 1882. The family left the eastern part of the state on their westward trek on June 4th and arrived in the Black Hills on August 6th.28

In 1879, Mrs. Hunter felt that it was her place to be with her husband to aid him in the struggle for existence. She determined to join him but did not inform him of her decision until she was ready to leave.

She leased her Minneapolis home for a year and with the money received set out with her three children. The railroad ended at Bismarck, and from there it was necessary to travel by stage. The children were ill when she reached Bismarck so she determined to await the stage, that the children might be better prepared for the long, arduous trip.

In Bismarck, Mrs. Hunter, by good fortune, met George Northran, who for many years was special agent for the Homestake Mining Company, and Dave Holyman, merchant, also from Deadwood, who were well acquainted with her husband. They offered their assistance with the children along the lonely trail to Crook City. During the long trip, travelling night and day, they took turns helping the little family.

The trip was uneventful with one exception: when the driver received word of the approach of a band of Indians. However, they did not materialize. Mrs. Hunter was given a loaded fire-arm, as was each passenger, and was thus partially prepared for any emergency.

Her husband met the stage at Crook City. He took them to the sawmill about eight miles away where he had built a cabin for their home. Mrs. Hunter, weary from the long trip, lay down to rest, while the children, excited by their new surroundings and the great forest, ran out to play. When she awakened, Mrs. Hunter could not find them.

Every prospector and resident in the vicinity began a search which lasted through the night. In the morning, they were found unharmed, sitting on the edge of a cliff, the younger of the two girls sleeping with her head in the lap of the older. They had been frightened by two rough-looking men and ran in the direction they thought would take them to the cabin, but which led them deeper into the woods.29

At the age of nine [in 1877], she came to the Black Hills with her parents and sister. Mrs. Massie's father, C.W. Pettigrew, was a prosperous Glenwood, Iowa, merchant. He speculated on the corn market and lost nearly everything he owned in the panic of 1873. He took his wife and ten children to Jewel City (now Mankato) Kansas, where he homesteaded. Every year for three years grasshoppers descended in clouds and ate up every growing thing.

In those days the "Weekly Inter-Ocean" was the paper for grownups. "My father read about the gold rush in the Black Hills and decided to see what things were like up there," recalled Min. "There were twelve wagons in our caravan. We used mules, oxen and even milk cows to pull the wagons. It took us three months to reach Spearfish."

It was dry in 1877 and the brown grass covering Spearfish valley reminded Mrs. Massie's father too much of drought-ridden Kansas. "Some of the men went to Deadwood but my father and the rest did not want to earn their livings from mining; they wanted to farm and raise cattle. So they decided to push on from Spearfish and go to the Big Horn mountains of Wyoming."

The first night out of Spearfish was an experience Mrs. Massie related scores of times. The pioneers had just made camp near the present site of Beulah when they heard shots not far away. Two soldiers, who had been cutting hay, were killed by Indians. The Pettigrew party prepared for the attack, men were assigned posts, the women stood ready to do what they could.

As soon as possible, a pit was dug in the center of the circle formed by the wagons. Pits were also dug outside each wagon. The men occupied the outer fortifications while the nineteen women and children took refuge in the larger central pit.

"In the daytime the sun beat down on us and it was insufferably warm," recalled Mrs. Massie. "So the men put up a tent over our pit. That helped. Once in a while we could see the feathers of the Indians sticking up in the distance." ... For three nights and two days the redmen laid siege. When they didn't attack, the whites knew the Indians were not as numerous as they first feared. Finally, in the cover of darkness, two men made a break for Spearfish and help.... "Hearing the hoof beats of the rescuing party is one of the most pleasant sounds in my memory," admitted Mrs. Massie.

I was only really frightened once when the Indians had us corralled," she said. "It was while we were huddled in the pit. A gust of wind blew over the tent pole, which hit my arm. I let out a terrific shriek. I thought the Indians had me for sure, that time."

After that experience, Mrs. Massie's father and the others decided Spearfish was an attractive place despite the brown grass. "He built a cabin near the stockade and homesteaded on a ranch five miles up the valley." 30

    We find Suzie Lane sitting uncomfortably on a wooden seat in the covered wagon, very tired and worn out from all the bumps, and besides, the June sun of the South Dakota prairie was beating down furiously on Suzie's family. Suzie was seventeen years of age now and felt that she was quite a big girl. Suzie had one brother, named Billy, who was three. He was sitting on Suzie's lap crying himself to sleep. Suzie's mother was worn out, too. It would soon be dark and time to make camp for the night.

    Suzie's dad walked along by the oxen trying his hardest to make them go faster. That was impossible, thought Suzie. The journey was getting rough and tiresome, too. Suzie liked it, though. You see, the wagon train behind them had an eighteen-year-old boy in it, and Suzie had gotten acquainted with him fast. Some nights Suzie would get up out of her so-called bed at the bottom of the covered wagon and give a silent whisper for the boy to come and talk to her. This was a pleasure toward which each day she would plan.

    For nights that went on. One night Suzie was sneaking along to go after Don, the boy from the next covered wagon, when all of a sudden out from behind the bushes came a fairly big-built person. Suzie was terrified, frozen to her spot. Finally a voice said, "Suzie, where are you?" Suzie gave a sigh of relief. "Oh, Don, I was scared to death. I thought it was an Indian or something," said Suzie. That night Suzie was so frightened she could not find courage to stay long at their meeting place.

    For months the train rode on. Usually there was one certain cook to cook for the whole band of people, but on this train of wagons there were five or six cooks. Sam was the most liked. He was short and fat and loved to pull jokes on others. One night Sam was making bread and instead of putting a dash of salt in it he poured a half cup of pepper in. Sam started sneezing. The joke was on all of them that day.

    One day on their journey they saw Indians. Suzie and her brother were quite frightened, but they soon found out the Indians only wanted to trade furs for guns, food and so forth. Suzie soon found that there was such a thing as friendly Indians.

Don helped Suzie's family with any difficulties that came up and the family appreciated it very much. In return they helped Don's family when possible.

Finally the day came when they came to the town of Deadwood in 1879. The families helped each other build log cabins and soon Deadwood became a very attractive little town. Quite often stagecoaches came through with people who stayed at the Inn called "Suzie and Don Wagner's Cozy Inn."31

Mrs. Emma A. Vickers' life, from the time she left Michigan, was interesting and eventful. A part of her journey to Lead from Michigan was by boat from Yankton to Pierre, an eight-day trip and the remainder of the journey, from Pierre to Lead, was by stagecoach in three days.

Mrs. Vickers came to South Dakota up the Missouri River from Yankton by boat. After a week of uncomfortable travel in an anything-but-luxurious river steamer, they landed at Pierre. In that day, Pierre was a roistering, frontier river town, and Mrs. Vickers said that she was frightened all of the time during the few days she was obliged to remain in the town. The river had been very low in that September, the passage had been slow, and time and again they had been stuck on sandbars, so she had missed the stage, and had to wait for the next one.

When the stage finally arrived, she began the long trip overland to the Black Hills. With the road scarcely more than a trail, it took two days to reach Rapid City. Mrs. Vickers said, as she heard people complain about the road between Pierre and Rapid in later years, that she always wanted to say, "Well, you should have been with me through the heat and dust of that September ride in the long ago, on that terrible stage trip, with my heart trembling with the fear that we might encounter either Indians or outlaws."32

With their small baby, Sarah, they came to the Black Hills in 1885 by ox team for Mrs. Weber's health. She remembered that the ox team ran away one day on their journey, a very unusual occurrence. Mrs. Weber was curious to see the oxen running, they being usually such slow animals, and went to the front of the wagon with her tiny baby in her arms.

Just then the wagon hit a bump, and the jolt almost threw the baby from her arms.33

Miss Elna Johnson received her education in Sweden, came to the United States by sail-boat with two brothers in the year 1869, worked as a domestic in Minneapolis, and married A. G. Anderson.

Mr. & Mrs. Anderson came to Dakota Territory in 1879, by ox-team from Minnesota with a herd of milk cows, to a ranch four miles north of Sturgis and Fort Meade, and two miles west of Bear Butte on Spring Creek. They sold milk to freighters and milk, butter and eggs to officers at Ft. Mead, Sturgis, Lead and Deadwood. Had a hard frontier life with fear of Indians.34

When the gold rush to the Black Hills began, Mrs. Rickel accompanied her parents, coming by oxen freight train to Deadwood in 1877. She was seventeen years of age. One year later, in 1878, she met and married Joe Rickel who had recently arrived from Indiana, also lured by the gold rush tales. They resided in lower Deadwood and were completely burned out by the Big Fire of 1879. This was a recession to the family as Mr. Rickle had made the furniture for the house and hardships were many.35

In 1880 the Goulette family came to the Black Hills in a covered wagon. There were six wagons in the train that left Glenwood, Iowa, on April 25 and arrived in Lead City, June 11, 1880.

Mrs. Mossing says, "Of course the journey to the Hills in 1880 was quite perilous. Because we were afraid of Indians, the men put the wagons in a circle at night and slept on the ground to keep watch". However, they did not encounter any Indians.36

"I was born in Cairo, Illinois, where my father had a grocery store and later moved into the Post Office. His Doctor urged him to go farther north or west as he had malaria, and yellow fever was soon to be his doom if he did not obey. Soon mother and I went to Yankton, South Dakota, to visit my uncle who was teaching in Yankton College. We stayed there while father was getting settled."

He finally reached the Black Hills where his sister came as the bride of a pioneer druggist, C.C. Bent, and arrived the night before the "big Deadwood Fire" which took most of the town. Their house was on the spot where the Christian Science Church now stands. He helped to put wet blankets and quilts on the roof to save the house. No fire departments existed then. Finally Father sent for us in June, 1880. We went from Yankton to Pierre by boat, and there arrangements had been made to join a large wagon train to the Black Hills and our destination, Deadwood.

The owner of an ox train had many wagons drawn by strong, sturdy oxen, yoked together by huge strong wooden yokes. The train was in sections, as oxen were trained to travel together. In the bottom of the wagons were flour and all sorts of food stuffs.

The train master's wife, Mrs. Whitney, and little boy, my age, had the leading wagon which freighted the most valuable things. Always the heaviest things were on the bottom; tarpaulins covered the cargoes and the passengers' bed rolls. Mrs. Whitney's little boy and I had much fun on the trip as we went very slowly.

Meals were prepared by camp cooks, who had wonderful meals, prepared over camp fires. The drivers of the oxen had long, rawhide whips to hurry the oxen along. But there wasn't much hurry in oxen.37

Mrs. Conners said that about all she can remember was being afraid of the Indians. They were in constant fear of an Indian attack. The wagon train traveled many times at night knowing the Indians wouldn't fight until day light which would be real early in the morning if they did attack at all. So they would make camp and keep close together. The women cooking, baking, and washing in the day time. They would be ready to travel again at night when they thought it necessary.38

John Baggaley started for the Black Hills in the spring of 1875 but was held at the Platte River because of government negotiations with the Indians. He returned to Galesburg and started again in the spring of 1877.

Mrs. Baggaley and their daughter, Mae, who was five years old, followed in September of the same year. They went by wagon train from Pierre. There were still frequent skirmishes with the Indians. A party had been wiped out the previous week. Every night, one man stood guard. The last night out from Deadwood, as no Indians had been seen on the trip, they decided to do without the night watch. Jennie Baggaley lay in the wagon with the flap of the wagon thrown back as the night was warm. The sky was clear, the moon shone brightly, and she thought the sky had never seemed so near. Suddenly above a rise of ground not far away, she saw the head of an Indian appear. She lay quietly for a moment, and then she saw a second head. She waited no longer, but slipped out of her wagon on the opposite side and aroused the men. They immediately set up guards and took every precaution for an attack. The Indians did not come closer and the next day they drove safely into Deadwood.39

      Katherina Merea Pohlzon. Such a big name for such a little girl! The family remedied that by calling me Katie. Born in Evanston, Wyoming, I was thoroughly Western. The first seven years were spent in Evanston, then, as now, a junction on the Union Pacific Railroad. My father was a tailor, and I, being a chatter-box, earned many a nickel by sitting absolutely still and quiet on Papa's press-board for five minutes, good training!

      In 1885 the lure of the Black Hills got Father. He left in February to establish a home in this Land of Promise at Rapid City. Mother and we three children followed in May, going by train to Sidney, Nebraska and the rest of the way by stagecoach. For three days and three nights we rode in the swinging coach -- stopping only a far cry from our present mode of travel.40

      Martin Johnson was a farmer, too. Though Iowa was good land, the times were filled with excitement. Gold in the west called like fever in the blood. In 1877, when he was twenty-seven, he and his brother Andy joined the westward-moving men and trekked into the Black Hills. They stayed over the winter, found it good, and in the spring went back after their families.
      It was not easy to leave Iowa. Two of Martin's and Annie's children, Oudolf and Gustava, were buried in the Decorah cemetery, dead before they had even half a chance to

grow up. Little George Richard was four years old; Rungdena was a baby.

They loaded a covered wagon with provisions, including two barrels of flour, one barrel of salt pork, one barrel of corned beef, a sack of navy beans and a sack of field peas, all paid by cash in advance. They had enough to last them two years, they figured. It was very provident of them, but too much. The horses couldn't haul it.

When they reached the Missouri River they had to make adjustments. Mrs. Johnson, George and Rungdena boarded one boat with the intention of waiting at Pierre for the men to join them in the wagon. The provisions were shipped on a second boat.

Then twice before they could catch their breath, tragedy struck the family. The boat carrying their provisions caught fire. Everything they had shipped was lost with an estimated $100,000.00 loss in cargo disappearing in smoke. The baby Rungdena died. How? We don't know. She was dead. Annie buried her little daughter at Pierre and was ready to join her husband again.

The freighter, Volin, was ferrying across the Missouri then. The covered wagon cost a five dollar fee, and the horses and cattle had to be ferried across, too. They joined a group of others who were going west.

In early June, the streams were running full, and the narrow trail across the state to the Black Hills crossed several water courses. The boy, Dick, remembered seventy-eight years later how they came to the Hills. Martin was a good swimmer. It was his task to swim across the creeks and get the team on the opposite bank. Once the horses were across, the wagon could be roped to the team and hauled through the water. Dick remembered that there were no brakes on that wagon. "The last time I made a trip I just thought, how in the world could they ever get up and down those mountains without brakes on the wagons," he reminisced. But they did.

It was a rough voyage. Often they were stopped for two or three days at a time because of high water. They reached Galena, booming silver camp south of Deadwood, on June 9, 1878.[41]

In 1877, Mrs. Granville Rockefeller rode into Deadwood on a stagecoach on her honeymoon trip. Fifty-two years later on a visit to the Black Hills, Mrs. Rockefeller again rode in the same stagecoach, an honored guest of the Days of '76 Committee. Times and ways have changed between the dates of those two trips, but Mrs. Rockefeller still clearly recalls the incidents of the days when she came to the Hills as a bride.

She was married to Granville Rockefeller on January 1, 1877, at Columbus, Nebraska, and left via train for Sidney. Rockefeller was superintendent of the stage line between Sidney and Deadwood. The line was owned by Marsh and Stevenson of Omaha. The newlyweds started for the Hills on the day following their wedding. It required eight days to make the trip which can now be made in less than twenty-four hours. The storms and blizzards delayed them and the fear of the Indians did not add to the enjoyment of the occasion but one wonders if perhaps these young people just embarking on the sea of life were not more interested in each other than in the perils and dangers of the road.

Early in 1875 Granville Rockefeller, clothed in a dress suit and patent leather shoes, had left Albany, New York, expecting to make a fairly quick trip to the Black Hills. He arrived at Columbus, Nebraska, and remained there until the spring of '76 when the government opened the Hills to the miners. He joined the well known "stampede company", which was composed of men who were eager to reach the land of wealth and luxury as quickly as possible. He paid $65.00 to join the company with the expectation of riding all the way but the wagons were so heavily laden that the men were forced to walk the entire distance of 300 miles. It took them nearly two months because of heavy storms. At night each man took his turn standing guard against the Indians. The other members of the company called Rockefeller the "Tenderfoot" because of his once-shiny patent leather shoes.

A short time after his arrival in Deadwood, volunteers were called to bring the mail and important messages from Sidney by pony express. The mail had been coming by ox train, the "overland freight" which used from twenty to forty yoke of oxen and required from two to six months to make the trip.

The people were dissatisfied with this slow mail service and the government posted notices asking for men to carry the mail on horseback. The sum of $100.00 was paid for the round trip and it took two weeks. Rockefeller volunteered and was accepted and thus became the first pony express rider in Deadwood. He rode by day and slept by night, tying his bridle rein to his wrist so that his horse might warn him of approaching danger, for a number of riders had previously been killed by the Indians. He was chased by them several times but always managed to outwit them.42

      She was only four years old when she arrived in Deadwood with her parents, in March 1876. Allen brought in the first stagecoach, she said, coming from Cheyenne. Allen owned a race track in Cheyenne. He came to the Black Hills in '74 and again in '75 but the military wouldn't let him stay.

      The trip took nearly three weeks and Indians twice attacked the stagecoach with its nineteen passengers. The Allen family lived at Central City for several years. Allen went into the livery stable business there.43

      Mrs. Belle Parker came at the age of four from Cheyenne, Wyoming by stagecoach, March 9, 1876 to Central City. It took nineteen days to reach her destination. There were nineteen in the party. The stagecoach was chased by the Oglala Sioux close to the Custer Stockade. The Cavalry was out scouting for the Indians when they saw them chasing the stage. They chased the Indians off. They said that the Indians wouldn't attack out in the open.

      Her father was already living here in a log house. He had a livery stable. He came on the first stagecoach that came into the hills when they signed the peace treaty with the Indians. He came for his business and for gold. They had bull teams in her days. On their way home with her father the bull teams got stuck in the mud on the road between Deadwood and Central City. While they were waiting for the team to get out she played in the mud.

      The first night in her new home was exciting. The bed on which she was to sleep was placed over a red ant pile.44

Women Homesteading on their Own

A chance to make an independent life, necessity, proving-up and then selling the land for profit -- there were a number of reasons why women homesteaded. Here are some of them.

In 1910, I filed on a homestead in Pennington County, eight miles southwest of New Underwood. I taught the rural school in the district and the next year taught in the grades at New Underwood. Proved up on the claim in fall of 1912. Returned to Irene and taught a year in Turner County.45

It happened that the man I was to marry had taken land a mile north of where Mitchell now stands. It is located in a beautiful valley with the Fire Steel Creek running through it. We were married and built our home on his homestead and there my child was born. Misfortune overtook us and my husband passed away in an insane asylum. My child was two years of age. For many years I worked hard to support myself and child for we were left destitute. I educated her and she became a school teacher. When she became twenty-one years of age, Meade County was opened for settlement, and we both came to the Black Hills in December of 1911, and both took up land side by side. She taught school at Cottonwood that winter, and I procured employment in Rapid City.46

In 1926 her husband died, but she "stuck to the farm." A lot of the time she was by herself there and continued to manage it until the years piled up when she realized it was too much for her, so she sold the land, but kept the house. 47

Laura Ann Kinchelo Dickinson came to Dakota Territory in 1883 from Parkensburg, West Virginia to join her sons. Her husband, Richard W. Dickinson, died in Missouri City, Missouri, during the Civil War. Mrs. Dickinson and her three daughters Rose, Harriet and Carnie arrived in the Black Hills by Stage coach in 1883.48

Mrs. Ashe worked in stores after she finished her education, and managed the Seebicks store for some years. But she also had a taste of the rugged side of life.

While very young she took a preemption claim near Aladdin, Wyoming, but some land hungry individual "jumped" it, so she filed on another, and had a log cabin on it. "I'd go out there and sleep often enough to hold it. I had to take a lot of razzing about it but managed to prove up on the land. I still own that land along with other land holdings and the income from it comes in handy now," said the genteel little lady.

But her experience homesteading is scarcely in the running when compared to her venture in building a house.

"Father gave each of us girls a lot, and I was the only one who built a house. At the time I was working for the staggering sum of $15.00 a month. I guess I built the house on hot air and promises," she laughed, remembering.

But luck smiled on her when a chance came to rent the house for $17.50 a month and she made it pay for itself.

"I didn't bother to have a foundation put under the house. The thing was stuck up on wooden stilts. Later I put a foundation under it when I could finance it," she recalled. 49

She, then Mrs. George Harvey, came to this part of the country from Nebraska in 1890. They arrived on Easter Sunday at what is now Provo. However, there wasn't a single building there at that time, nor for that matter, were there any at Edgemont or Hot Springs. Only one acre of barren land. It was here that they homesteaded.

Upon the death of her husband a short time later, this plucky little pioneer carried on alone, braving the elements, the Indians who were troublesome, and worst of all, the gray wolves. These pests were so plentiful and so vicious one never dared be caught on the prairie off his horse. And they boldly slaughtered calves in broad daylight. The Texas Longhorn cattle, in which they specialized, were also a constant source of fear.

In due time our little lady married Mr. O. B. Williams, a western cowboy. Their life on the ranch continued. During this time she frequently administered to the sick. Astride a horse, she would ride as much as seventy-five miles to bring a baby into the world. There were no doctors, and no nurses, and she was not one to shirk what she felt to be her duty.50

In the spring of 1878 they came to Buffalo Gap, Dakota Territory thence to Rapid City, Dakota Territory in the spring of 1880, to Keystone, South Dakota in 1901 and then to Wind Cave National Park in 1910, where Mr. Boland died in 1912. After her husband's death, Mrs. Boland "proved up" on a homestead in Carter County, Montana.

Eight children were born to Mr. and Mrs. Boland, all deceased except John A. and William M., who reside at Rapid City, South Dakota. Mrs. Boland was active in her church (Episcopal) and gave a great deal of her life to the care of the sick and afflicted, especially during the early days at Rapid City and Keystone, when there were no nurses or hospitals and few doctors.51

Mary Pinney Murphy is one of the original "Liberated Women." She came with her family from Desching, Czechoslovakia to [Taben], South Dakota. When she was only a few months old. Her family settled three-and-one-half miles northeast of New Underwood, and Mary and her sister and three brothers grew up there going to school when it was available, and helping on the Homestead the rest of the time. Since her older sister helped in the house, and her brothers helped with the crops, it was Mary's job to keep track of the cattle, which roamed on open range. Mary went to St. Martin's Academy in Rapid City for her high school education. After her graduation in 1905, at nineteen, she became a bookkeeper at Meyer's Store in Sturgis. She worked there two years, and managed the store when the owner went on vacations or business trips. She saw no future in [Ohio], and took a homestead when she was twenty-one, in 1908, near Wasta. To make a living for herself, she taught school for six months in new Underwood, then five months in Caputa, and commuted to her homestead on weekends. Mary met her husband-to-be, Paul Cornelius Murphy, when he took up a homestead adjoining hers, and they were married in Rapid City, January 26, 1910.52

She, then Mrs. George Harvey, came to this part of the country from Nebraska in 1890. They arrived on March 13,

Easter Sunday, at what is now Provo. However, there wasn't a single building there at that time, nor for that matter, were there any at Edgemont or Hot Springs. Only one acre of barren land. It was here that they homesteaded on the land which is now a part of the Black Hills [Ordnance] Depot.

Upon the death of her husband a short time later, this plucky little pioneer carried on alone, braving the elements, the Indians who were troublesome, and worst of all, the gray wolves. These pests were so plentiful and so vicious one never dared be caught on the prairie off his horse. And they boldly slaughtered calves in broad daylight. The Texas Longhorn cattle, in which they specialized, were also a constant source of fear.

In due time our little lady married Mr. O. B. Williams, a western cowboy. Their life on the ranch continued. During this time she frequently administered to the sick. Astride a horse, she would ride as much as seventy-five miles to bring a baby into the world. There were no doctors, and no nurses, and she was not one to shirk what she felt to be her duty.53

My mother, Olive Railsback, grew up a Christian and a temperance advocate. She was married to my father, James Brown, in Ottawa, Iowa. He was a person of high ideals and habits of Christian Integrity. Having been born in April 1849 the "gold fever" was in his veins. His restlessness made him a poor man; but the fact that the first twenty years of married life brought twelve babies to live with them (only one died in early infancy) he never realized his dream of a "home in Sunny California," until he became ill and was persuaded to seek surgical aid in a Hospital in Turlock, California where he was presently living. He died on the table, though the operation was not considered of special danger.

My mother lived on, on the homestead they had filed soon after their arrival in Dakota Territory. My father came from Atlantic, Iowa, in March 1879, and mother with five small children came later by train from Atlantic where we boarded a flat-bottomed steamer, which brought us comfortably to Pierre, in July 1880. From there we took a mule team and covered wagon to the Black Hills.

My mother was a sturdy little Pennsylvania Dutch type. Honest integrity was her life, and as a devoted Christian, she held her children strictly to the teachings of the Holy Bible. Though she had but little chance of schooling, she always found means to improve her education, having a goal set to give each of her children a college education. One made it. Her devotion and great ability would make a glowing adventure story, but I am seventy-seven, am not able to do it justice. 54

Clara Kuntz Jarvis, with her husband and the five oldest of their ten children, who lived her whole life within three miles of her girlhood home.

Once Here

The trip was over. What had they come to? In many cases, land they couldn't claim, because the government had only recently taken it from the Lakota and hadn't yet surveyed it. Still, they built their houses and stayed. It was often a long way into town, and, until the mail-order catalog made its entrance, the peddler provided an important community service.

Clara Kuntz Jarvis came to Pleasant Valley, Meade County, in 1882 and still lives in the Valley, the only one left of the original early settlers of Pleasant Valley.

There being no school in that neighborhood, Mrs. Jarvis was nine years old before she began her formal education. Her father gave an acre of land on which that first school, called the Harlow School, was built.

He sold his homestead and bought the Hoehn place, only three miles from Mrs. Jarvis' girlhood home. Here they raised ten children in the same old house. Mr. Jarvis passed away in 1938 but Mrs. Jarvis still lives on the home place with her two youngest sons, farming and raising livestock.55

At the time they moved to the Dakota Territory they were among the first white settlers in this part of what is now Fall River County. They settled here before the land was surveyed, locating as "squatters", and filing a pre-emption claim as soon as a survey was made, and later changing it to a homestead. 56

The first summer was spent establishing residency and proving up on a pre-emption claim on Spring Creek, near Hermosa. Farm land was the bonanza that was to make millionaires of all of us. Father didn't make it.

The next five summers we proved up on a homestead claim twelve miles East of Rapid City. One of the family's treasured documents is the patent to this 160 acres of farm land, signed by United States President Benjamin F. Harrison, January 30, 1892.57

In those days, when pioneers couldn't get to town for long periods of time, they didn't worry much. Peddlers, traveling the dim buckboard trails in spring wagons, were plentiful and they supplied the needs. It was an event when a peddler lighted from his spring wagon and headed towards our house with a big pack on his back. They had everything from mousetraps on up, including jewelry, shirts and long-handled undies. As the years moved along, the peddlers became less numerous because many of them (who were generally Syrians), settled in small stores in Deadwood."58

"We used to have to order our spring supplies in the fall in order to have them in time. And just think -- now we often get orders within five days time."59

Eventually, however, they arrived at a place on Indian creek, which they all thought would be a good location for a home. They immediately set about building a log house. The house was made of peeled cottonwood logs, notched at the ends to hold them together, about sixteen feet wide, by forty feet long, with two glass windows. Glass windows were a luxury at this time and had to be hauled all the way from Crawford, Nebraska. 60

Anna Jackson's first home in Dakota was located along the beautiful Fall River, about two miles southeast down the canyon from the youthful town of Hot Springs. Her father built a three-room log cabin with a sod roof. She recalled, "We used the water from Fall River for drinking and cooking. It was crystal clear and good." 61

In 1890, she came out to Whitewood on a visit. Maybe there was an ulterior motive as she had a sweetheart on a horse ranch at Macy, forty miles north of Belle Fourche. His name was Fred Ernest and the young couple married that fall and set up housekeeping in "a two-room dugout with a cellar going on back." There wasn't even a floor in the dugout until about time for the bride to arrive when everybody got busy and put in a floor of wide pine boards. Their furniture was pretty meager and the cupboards were home-made.

The young couple soon abandoned the dugout, which was cozy, and built a lovely home with eight rooms. It was made of lumber hauled from the old Whitcomb's sawmill with Ernest as contractor, chief, head carpenter and crew!

Inside of the house was finished with "double L" muslin made nice and smooth, then kalsomined. Ernest made all the doors and designed and built an outside woodbox which opened into the kitchen. The kitchen had plenty of built-ins. 62

"We had a sod house on our claim. They used walking plows then and to 'throw up' a sod house the land was plowed and chunks of sod was laid up a good deal like they lay a brick wall. I guess the sod chunks or slabs were about twenty-four inches long by sixteen inches wide. Our neighbors helped us build and the house was fourteen by twenty, all in one big room."

"It was plastered inside and was warm in winter and cool in summer, and it had a good rubberoid roof, too. You can tell it was well-built as it stood for twenty-five years." 63

Mrs. Small recalls that housekeeping in those days was quite different from what it is now. She carried water from a barrel at the back door which was filled about once a week. Light was furnished by kerosene lamps; wood and coal were used for cooking and heating. She baked her own bread and ironed with flat irons heated on the stove.64

The first home (frame) of Mr. and Mrs. P.A. Gushurst consisted of two (12x12) rooms. There was no insulation in these early homes, no plaster and a single floor. Later a shed kitchen was added. As conditions changed and the family increased, the house (except for the first two rooms which were later made into one) was added to and subtracted from, several times. It finally developed into a house of ten rooms, two bathrooms, basement and steam heated.65

"Our house was built of logs. It had the largest room of any house in the country, so it was more or less a community center." 66

On March 23, 1878, they reached the home on Redwater that Mr. Davis had prepared. There was two feet of snow on the ground. Mrs. Davis was pleased with the new log home which had matched flooring and a shingled roof. Many early settlers had only the ground for a floor, or wide boards and roofs of slabs. 67

They built a one-room cabin with a lean-to on it. The furniture consisted of a table, some benches, and a built-in bunk. It was all made of rough lumber. For heat and cooking there was only a steel, cast-iron stove. They carried water from where the ruins of the Hearst Mercantile are now.
Mrs. Ballantyne had a large, grand, square piano brought in by the bull train. She had a sewing machine and made her clothes. The plate glass for the windows was brought in by bull train. The glass now costs more to be sent in by train than it did then to be sent in by bull train. 68

"We lived in a two-room, two-story house with a dirt cellar. There were eight of us, my parents, five children and our grandfather. " 69

John Baggaley had built the cabin which was to be their first home in the Black Hills at a settlement back of White Rocks called Twobit. At this point they were finding some very large nuggets. John was not an experienced woodsman, and he did not bark the logs he used in building the cabin. As a result, a countless number of bedbugs abode with them.
One afternoon, Jennie walked over the hill to show Mrs. Hardin how little Maud was growing. Mae was at school with the other children. It was a pleasant day, and the two friends had a cup of tea and enjoyed a long visit. When Jennie returned, she found their cabin burned to the ground. Nothing was left but a small iron stove her father had sent with her and two sand irons. What she mourned for most was a Seth Thomas clock she had brought with her and a good mother cat and her three little kittens. The next cabin John built he cleaned logs, and there were no more bedbugs. But without the good cats, the mice gave them much trouble.70

Their first home was a dugout on their homestead in the "Jump Off" country. The walls were finished inside by hanging burlap over the sod. One night rattlesnakes could be heard in the walls and they were afraid to go to bed. One particular time when the bedding had been aired on the ground a rattlesnake was carried inside their home.71

The big boom in 1876, when the Boylans moved into South Dakota, was toward Deadwood, and to Deadwood William Boylan brought his wife and two small children. William settled his family in a home, and finding most of the mining claims already taken, went to Keystone about fifty miles distant in the southern part of the Black Hills and tried to mine. He was no miner, and finally admitted it to himself and the world. He had a team of mules and a wagon, so hauled freight between Custer, Keystone, Deadwood and Fort Meade, joining his family at Deadwood whenever the opportunity arose.

Jennie's and William's third child was born in Deadwood, Stella, with the claim to fame of being the second child born in Deadwood. As soon as she could, Jennie began to work on odd jobs while William was away freighting. Later she worked as a cook for Joe Broad's sawmill gang. Joe Broad was a sawyer with an eye to history, and with the first tree that went through his mill he constructed a table and a cupboard -- the first boards ever sawed in Deadwood.

William's brother Jim, and his wife, Mary, followed them to the Black Hills, and Jim settled on some good land near Piedmont about thirty miles southeast of Deadwood. William decided to homestead near Jim. In 1880, he drove his mules and wagon into Deadwood, picked up his wife Jennie and the three children, and headed back down the hills to the homestead lands upon which he had filed near Piedmont. Joe Broad gave Jennie the table and cupboards built from his first tree as a gift to help the young couple get started again on housekeeping. Today in 1956 that table is still on the family lands, and the cupboards are used in the bunk house.

William built a log house on the lowlands. About the first thing that happened was a flash flood that washed the log house away. Undaunted, he made plans for a stone house higher on the hill, but before he could begin that he had to build a rock foundation for a barn. The Boylans lived in that rock-based barn for two or three years while William worked carefully on the stone house. When he was through he had a home that stands today, over seventy years, later as strong and steadfast as it did the day he finished it.72

Agnes Ann came to South Dakota under rather odd circumstances. She had met and fallen in love with William F. Long, while visiting a sister who was teaching and boarding at the Long home in Canada. They had even talked of marriage. There was a distance of some fifty miles between homes in those days (1875) and it was like going around the world today in a jet. He eventually met and married another young woman.

In 1891 he, having lost his wife and one young son in the smallpox epidemic there, picked up his widowed mother and three small children (including a six-month-old baby girl) and came to Vale, where a brother-in-law had taken up a homestead.

It was there that my mother came in '97. After renewed acquaintance via letter, William went back to Marmora and brought her back. There were three young children to greet her (the youngest six years old) to which later four more were added. Faced with seven youngsters and no facilities as we have, she rolled up her sleeves and made one of the most marvelous lives for the whole family, including hired help, both in and out of the house. And she was always ready to help the neighbors. 73

Her father squatted on land on Box Elder Creek. They camped in Dark Canyon for the first year, getting out logs for their cabins and barns. When the buildings were completed, they moved out to Box Elder Creek about five miles from Rapid City. The land that they squatted on was about one-and-one-half miles from the Pierre to Black Hills wagon trail. We would sit on the doorstep and watch the wagon trains, pulled by oxen, plod along the well-worn trail.

Once, in the first few months of living on the land, we were out of flour and couldn't buy any at Rapid City so father went to the wagon trail and managed to buy from a freighter, twenty-five pounds of corn meal for $5.00 for the two families of us who had shared with one another until there was nothing left to share.

We had plenty of wild game: deer, antelope, and buffalo. My father did much trading with the Indians. We often ate with them and after the meal the men all took turns smoking the "Peace Pipe." I remember the Lakota women putting a back protection on their children to keep their backs straight and strong. It was made of stout buffalo hide and moulded to fit and cover a baby's back and sides from shoulder to hip.74

An uncle's determination to return to the Black Hills where he had once lived spread to the Hough family and April 1, 1882, with covered wagon behind a yoke of oxen, they set out. They now had six children ranging in age from eighteen months to thirteen years. There were several wagons in the caravan and the older children helped drive the cattle all the way through. They had difficulty in driving through some very bad sloughs and had to dispose of some heavy iron utensils and some other things to lighten the load. They encountered a number of Indians but were not molested. It was hard driving through the creeks and crossing the Cheyenne River.

Finally in June, two months after starting from northwest Iowa, they pulled into mud-soaked Deadwood. Through the town they went and on to Brownsville -- here Mr. Hough worked for a time in the lumber mill. Then on to Centennial Prairie where they worked on a farm. Mrs. Hough took in sewing and did considerable washing.

Later they started ranching on Pleasant Valley and here was labor indeed -- the family built its own home, dug a well, plowed the soil and sowed crops. Two winters they moved to Rapid City to send the children to school; here their second boy was born.

In the spring of 1888 they sold their place and rented a farm four miles north of Sturgis, bought cows, and besides raising crops and chickens, sold milk to the creamery. The seven years they lived here were full of cares, hard work, and vicissitudes of life. Mrs. Hough proved herself a hero through all their hardships. She said the only way to do was to look on the bright side and go ahead.75

So, they started on, headed for the Black Hills. They camped on the bank of Hat Creek, almost where the creek empties into the Cheyenne River August 1, 1885. Here they made their last camp together. Andy was so well-pleased with his location, he soon made claim to this land. They staked their claim and built up their homes. It was called a Squatter Right. Later years the land was surveyed, and each one was given a title to his land.76

The door of the Rail ranch house was never locked and any traveler who happened to pass by was always welcome at the Rail table or to spend the night. "We never turned away anyone," recalls Mrs. Rail. Sometimes leaves were added to the long table to make beds for the children when visitors occupied the youngsters' beds. Once a lawyer, a doctor, a priest, and an undertaker were seated around the family table. They just happened to drop by about the same time and, of course, were invited to stay.77

Mrs. Gushurst came to the Black Hills in 1877 with her uncle, Fred Manual, who with his brother, Moses, discovered the Homestake lode. Gushurst came to the Hills in 1876 to prospect for gold and went into the mercantile business. On August 15, 1876, he established the first grocery store in Lead.78

Mabel Grace Cachelin Wolfe was born in Spearfish in 1881 "with bullets flying over her head".

The Wild West

Lawless and wild, or chivalrous and respectful -- markedly varied were the Black Hills women's experiences of the cowboys who trailed cattle up from Texas into the rich pastureland when this area was still open range.

Another incident occurred one night when the town was full of cowboys drinking whisky and shooting. They would mount their horses and ride full-speed up and down Main Street, yelling and shooting straight for the sky usually, but this night there was a heavy rainstorm and Mother went to the show window to remove some pattern hats, when a bullet whizzed through the window, just escaped her, and landed in the side wall of the building. So much of Pioneer Life. 79

Those were the years of the cowboys and roundups. As there were no Inns or Travelers homes, there were many cowboys and settlers stopping at the ranches for meals and overnight, so they were busy days for the ranchers and their wives. We were never afraid as they respected women and children, even though they often came with six-shooters strapped to their belts and spurs on their boots.80

Mabel Grace Cachelin, the youngest daughter of Edward Cachelin and Columbia Dotson Cachelin, was born in a little white house on the corner of Jackson Street, December 23, 1881 at Spearfish, South Dakota, in Lawrence County. With bullets flying over their heads, the tiny baby and her mother were nearly killed by cowboys riding in "to shoot up the town".81

The first night in the hotel in Spearfish was eventful. Horsemen rode into the hotel and shot up into the ceiling. They were searching for a gang of horse thieves. 82

While their lives were kept separate from the "bad girls," the Black Hills pioneer women stood fascinated by the prostitutes and notorious (quickly legendary) characters who followed the trail of lawlessness into the Black Hills:

While Deadwood was reputed to be wild and woolly, Mrs. Rail said "a lady was perfectly safe there -- I never once was insulted." She and other "respectable" people never paid any heed to what those in the other half -- "the badlands" -- did. But there was at least a "nodding" recognition when the good ladies passed the bad on Deadwood's Main Street. "Everybody always spoke to one another." 83

"We had to go right through Chinatown and there were lots of Chinese there in those days. We girls were never afraid, though. As far as actual roughness, I don't think Deadwood was as rough then as it is now. Many well-known people lived in the First Ward."

"Girls dressed more modestly then. Why, we couldn't have gone around in overalls, shirt tails flying the breeze as they do now. I recall one man dressmaker and milliner in those years. He made fine clothes, and most of our cloth was imported. I still have one of my imported dresses, and the cloth was expensive."

"We put on plenty of style in those years. When the Opera house opened, the ladies had evening gowns and opera cloaks for the affair. It was quite an event."

"Of course, as you've often heard, there were lots of saloons, and gambling places. Plenty of rough characters drifted in, but they seemed to keep their places," said the frail little lady. 84

She said Deadwood was very wild and wooly. There was hardly a night that you didn't hear shooting. There were clear streams of water running down the streets. She saw Calamity Jane walking down the streets in Deadwood.85

"In those early years Hill City had three saloons, and there was a "Bismarck Annie" in Hill City. She had a "fancy house" and was the madam. She was the talk of the town and scandalized the whole community."86

On our arrival, we found many good, hard-working citizens, and they, like us, were seeking new homes. Besides these, there were cowboys, soldiers, freighters, gold-seekers, and lots of dancehall girls and gamblers at Sturgis.

Some of the more exciting characters that I remember were Madame Bull Dog, Baldy Ford, Doc. Linch and Calamity Jane. I remember Madame Bull Dog only once, a nice-looking woman, who ran a sort of camping place for travelers between here and Rapid City. She owned two huge, fierce-looking bull dogs. It was rumored that some of her stoppers were never seen again, and she, herself, finally disappeared as mysteriously as she had lived. 87

"We were not even allowed to walk along the street past the old Bodega as that part of the town was pretty wild. I grew up in Deadwood and went to school there and finished high school. I recall that I used to sit beside Belle Parker in school," said Mrs. Berry.

"As for historic characters that gave Deadwood its reputation, I'll mention only one. Preacher Smith, who tried to do some good, and the men like the fathers of some of us pioneer women who are the descendants of good men who tried to keep the churches going and the schools for children and to keep the wickedness down. Politics then were run by the saloon-keepers. At least I saw a great deal of wickedness going on in "Historic Deadwood", in spite of it.

"And Sturgis was plenty rough in those days, too. Riff-raff seemed to float in from everywhere, and we had sixteen saloons at one time. A woman wasn't safe to walk along the streets at night."88

Not a single account of the omnipresent gambling establishments finds its way into the women's stories. Not surprising, since a woman entering through the door would immediately and irreparabl sully her reputation. The only gambling description comes from a husband:

"I've seen most all these better buildings you see here now come into being since I came here," said Ole. "In the gambling halls -- and there were plenty of them here -- I've often seen as high as $10,000 stacked right in sight on the table. Just try to imagine that. The Chinese were all great gamblers, too.89

Murder was a way of life; horse thieves were hung.

Scott was delayed for a month by a severe storm at Sidney. Every day, Mrs. Scott relates, as he returned to his room from his meals, he met four men, always together. He met them again at Custer, where one of them, the youngest, tried to get Scott to join them, which he declined to do. They went on to Rapid City and later stole some horses. They were pursued by a posse, which overtook them when they were asleep. The youngest (who had tried to induce Scott to join them), started to run, but his overalls dropped down over his pantaloons so that he couldn't run, and the posse nabbed him. The thieves were placed in Scott's barn and afterwards hanged on Hangman's Hill. Local historians say the young man was innocent, but Mrs. Scott declared he was guilty, as he was with the other men a whole month at Sidney.90

Mother saw many of the historic events of the Black Hills area happen. As a child she saw "Lame Johnny", notorious Hills outlaw, the night of July 1, 1879, when he was taken from a stagecoach and hanged on the banks of the creek which today bears his name. Grandma served him his last meal at the stage station operated by her uncle, George Boland, who later lived and died in Spearfish.

She saw "Lame Johnny" several times, and her uncle knew him very well. He was a little fellow with an unusually large mouth and walked with a limp. His real name was Cornelius Donahue and he took the alias John A. Hurley in the Black Hills. He was a college graduate, brought up in Pennsylvania and drifted into Texas, where the whites were having difficulty with the Indians stealing horses. "Lame Johnny" retaliated by running off bands of Indian horses and later came to the Black Hills.

For a time he worked for the Homestake Mining Company, but quit his job soon after a Texas acquaintance entered the office and pointed him out as a horse thief. He went back to his former dubious profession of stealing horses, making little distinction between those of whites and Indians, and finally, he and his gang robbed a stagecoach on "Lame Johnny Creek". He was later apprehended and was being taking to Deadwood for trial when a group of men, whose names are not known, seized him and hanged him to a tree.91

Sturgis:
Baldy Ford was found buried in the sand with a rope around his neck. He was reputed to have imported many dance hall girls.
The incident of the shooting of Dr. Linch by a African-American soldier, caused great excitement and fear in the town. The African-American was hung west of town and on that night, all lights were out, and everyone ordered indoors, as the African-American infantry had threatened to raid the city. 92

Spearfish:
"The first Sunday, we climbed Lookout Mountain, and the next Sunday we visited the cemetery. Seven were buried there, then. Off-hand, I'm not sure I can remember all of them. There were the two Rhodes' children, and a sister of Minnie Massie who was drowned in Spearfish creek, a man who was frozen to death in a blizzard, and Beans Davis (he was hanged by the vigilantes)."
"In those days, you could get away with killing a man when you couldn't, with stealing a horse or cow. Beans and his partner were caught and hanged on the other side of Lookout for stealing cattle. Maybe the grave beside him was his partner -- I'm not sure. The other grave could have been that of a young man killed by Indians out near Beulah."
"There hadn't been anyone killed right in Spearfish up to the time we moved [1878-1883]. That winter, four or five were killed. There was Harry Tuthill, who was hanged, and one of the sporting-house girls. She's buried in Deadwood; I've seen her grave."93

Hill City:
"One day a stagecoach went by and I saw two men fighting on top. One man slid off into a big willow tree and the coach went ahead as if they didn't even miss him. Mother and I went down to see if he needed anything or if we could get help for him. But he was gone, so he must not have been hurt much, I guess."

Lead had no notorious activity like Deadwood. There were no robberies and houses were all left unlocked until after the railroad came.94

"And talk about drinking in this day and age," said this little pioneer who is a good talker. "It was so common in those days we would often come across a man lying dead-drunk in the street. There were lots of rough characters travelling through or else just floating around."
The pioneers had plenty of close brushes with criminals. Mrs. Mills says a man stayed all night at their house once and had a nightmare in the night. He talked aloud about having killed somebody. We always did think he was wanted for wife-murder as there had been such a case.

"Another day a tramp came along and stopped at our house. He had parts of handcuffs on! But he was hungry, so, of course, we fed him, as we always did. He ate almost a whole pan of hot biscuits as if he were starved. He was in a terrible hurry and left as soon as he put the biscuits away."95

"Nothing ever bothered us in the woods", Mrs. Nelson said, "There were a few rattlesnakes in some places and once we saw a fox. We even heard that while he was picking berries a man called Raspberry Bill was killed by someone who had a grudge against him".96

"I recall the time a man named Brown killed a woman with a hatchet in the basement behind a cafe -- I think that was where the VFW is now. You maybe could tell even yet, for years and years there was a mark on the floor made by the hatchet. I bet if you look it's still there.
Justice was swift -- and Brown was hanged by authorities. The hills of Deadwood swarmed with people watching the hanging in the old courthouse yard. Matt Plumbet was sheriff then."97

Food

Food meant survival, and the land was a good provider. Eating off the land, a sense of bountiful plenty replaced fear, even when money was tight and the rains didn't come. The family sold whatever they raised beyond what they needed.

"With all the milk and butter we wanted, plenty of meat and eggs and all our own vegetables, the living cost never worried us at all."98

Soon he was cultivating 100 acres of valley land and raising remunerative crops of grain and vegetables. Wild berries and fruits grew profusely in the region, and the family gathered wild raspberries, blackberries, service berries, strawberries, and wild plums and cherries. "We were rich," says Mrs. Scott, "in eatables." The next summer after their arrival on Battle River, they were selling vegetables to people in the Rockville mining camp and earning a profitable income.99

I helped Mother gather eggs, set the hen and raise the baby chicks, ducks, geese and turkeys. We had a time trying to keep the little ducks off the pond until they were a few weeks old, because the muskrats would eat them when they were tiny. The coyotes would capture the little turkeys if their mothers took them too near the hills. And the hoot owls would come at night and steal the chickens if we left them in the yard -- not to mention the harm the skunks did. So, it really was a task for us to watch them all and do everything else. It was also our job to teach the young calves to drink milk.

Mother was very small, not over four feet and six inches tall, and I was small for my age, so we were afraid of the gander and the old turkey gobbler. The worst whipping I ever got was from the saucy old gander. He grabbed the front of my skirt and flopped his wings against the sides of my legs until they were black and blue. I was about to faint when Dad fought him off and he tried to attack him. Mother had a similar experience with the gobbler, who jumped and struck her in the back with his feet, breaking two settings of precious turkey eggs. From that time on, we carried a long stick or broom as our defense weapons and we really used them.

I believe the most interesting season of the year was in the fall when Mother and I filled the root house or cellar with the winter's supply of food. She canned fruits, vegetables and made all sorts of pickles, jellies and jams. I remember one year we had a huge barrel of dill pickles and they were delicious. When we ran out of jelly glasses, we took catsup bottles and tied a string, which had been soaked in kerosene, around the bottle and set it afire. As soon as it burned off we would strike the top of the bottle with a hammer and it would break off leaving a glass, which, when filled, was sealed with parawax and a paper cap.

At this time our home didn't have a basement and the root-house, or cellar, was some distance from the house and all this food had to be carried down there and placed on shelves. We used to have a large bin of potatoes, mounds of sand over carrots and parsnips, hubbard squash, pumpkins, a barrel of saurkraut, cabbage, onions and a box, or barrel, of apples. A lot of the different pickles were in open crock jars with a plate over the top and they never spoiled. We used to make pumpkin butter in the winter.

Mother would pick the warmest day possible to make a trip to this cave for a week's supply to fill the pantry. It always seemed like the deepest snow drift was in front of that cellar door. Father had two doors, one at the top of the stairs and one at the bottom. We had to carry a kerosene lantern and close the outside door before opening the inner door so there would be no danger of frost getting into the cellar. A heavy blanket was also hung in front of the inner door. Now, you can imagine what a task it was to get out with our load, and then, just compare it to our modern life with a basement and home freezer.100

We never thought of buying meat, for wild game was so plentiful that, whenever we needed meat, my father would just open the window or door and shoot a deer. We could look out any time of day and see antelope or deer near the house. Oftentimes hunters from Deadwood would come along and give us buffalo meat. They would come out with four-horse teams, kill a wagon load of meat and sell it to the butchers in Deadwood, making good money with the hides and meat. During the summer months, we jerked venison or buffalo meat and, once or twice, hunters gave us some bear meat but we could not relish this. It was always possible to raise a good garden and during fruit season we could can enough to last a year, so we had little to worry about, except to watch for rattlesnakes and bear while gathering fruit. The big "Brunos" liked berries, too. 101

    Berries of many kinds -- raspberries, strawberries, chokecherries, pincherries, oregon grapes and even white raspberries were found in the hills then. All these made delicious jellies, pies, or fruit for canning. Sometimes the children sold some of the berries, getting about a dollar for a ten-quart pailful.
    She still goes out in the hills in the summer and gathers berries and other fruit growing wild. Though berries aren't very plentiful now, Mrs. Nelson knows the hollows where they can be found. Last summer she gathered, and put up, about forty quarts of various kinds of wild fruit. 102

    "Our flour we always bought in 100-pound lots, as I baked all our bread and other bakery stuff we used, because it wasn't so easy to run out and buy bakery stuff like now." 103

    Until I was about six years old, we lived in a three-room house, plus a summer kitchen and a dirt cellar under the house. This cellar was very important because there wasn't any refrigeration and the cellar remained about the same temperature. The walls were dug so that they would not cave in. They were not cemented or walled-up with rock.
    My folks milked cows, as did all the neighbors, not with milking machines, but by hand. The milk was stored in this cellar until the cream raised. Then it was skimmed off by hand. Every so often the cream was churned and made into butter. Mother would spend hours, it seemed, washing this butter with a wooden-butter paddle to remove all the buttermilk. Then it was worked more to remove all the water and to mix in the right amount of salt. It was then shaped into pound amounts and wrapped.

Once a week, Dad would hitch up the team and take this butter, eggs, and maybe some other produce, drive twenty-five miles to Hot Springs, and sell the butter to customers. This was done during summer and winter. It was a hard life.104

Mrs. Emery's family bought their supplies by the wagonload. A big box of prunes cost about one dollar. In the winter time, they would bring two sleds with four head of horses, a wagon, not less than five hundred dollars worth at a time, only by the cases; it would be a whole winter's supply. 105

A widow writes: Life was simpler, even though in the early days she made all the butter consumed by her family and had some to sell. Getting fruit for canning and for jelly was a simple matter. It meant rounding-up her children and starting out, armed with pails.

They would come home with all the pails (and the children) filled with wild grapes, plums, chokecherries and buffalo berries. But finances were often a problem and Mrs. Carter would go help somebody out with their work to bring in some extra cash to help keep her family together.106

"I baked my own bread and made our butter. Coffee was ten cents a pound and Arbuckle was our favorite brand because it put out a set of map cards of the states. We used up barrels of coffee trying for a complete set of maps which were not plentiful or free in those days," she says.107

This Dry Creek area was a dairy community. Father and the hired man did the milking and fed the calves, but the milk skimming was done by hand and fell to mother's lot as did the printing of the butter. This was taken to Deadwood, fourteen miles to the southwest, every week in summer and on alternate weeks in winter. There was a garden to tend, chickens to look after, much cooking and washing and sewing for five, very small children. Mother usually had a hired girl but just now she had none. Christena stepped right in and helped with everything. 108

The Woods settled near Vale where Mr. Woods engaged in farming and ranching. "We took care of seven milk cows for a neighbor," Mrs. Woods recalled, "and we got part of the milk and butter as well as the heifer calves." 109

Deer and antelope were visible from the cabin door at most any time, so venison was easily obtained. Buffalo roamed mostly on the north side of the Belle Fourche River. There were large herds of the big shaggy beasts. Mr. Davis often went out in the morning with the team and wagon and returned at night with a load of buffalo meat which he sold in Deadwood. 110

In the spring of 1908, Mr. and Mrs. Comes moved to Cottonwood, where pioneer life was no gentler. The drought was so deep that when they planted seed in the ground, it did not even sprout. They used creek wood for heat and cooking, gathered buffalo berries and wild cherries, and somehow managed to make a living. 111

"I am still using the cookstove Bert bought in 1895, a WoodBine. It has been in constant use. It bakes as good today as any of the up-to-date new models."112

Wheat raised on one of the above farms won second prize at the St. Louis Expedition in the year 1902.113

"There's always something to eat in the ranch house," she declared. "But you always have to be running to the store if you live in town." 114

Water

The water was crystal-clear and pure, but away from the creeks, presented a problem: how to get it?

"We only milked two cows but I made all our butter. Water had to be hauled a mile which was the reason we didn't have more cows. We kept hogs for our own meat and sometimes sold one."115

There were hard times though, she recalls. Water was a major problem in the new little town. It had to be hauled down from the creek in barrels. She said, "The water was so nice and cold and tasted so good." But it wasn't easy for the young mother to drive the "stoneboat" to the creek for water when the husband was away at work. She was so happy, years later, when the water system was put in on the north side of town.116

Water, of course, was a problem. The water used for the boarding house had to be procured from down in the mine. It was brought up in barrels. Of course, someone had to go down on the cage, carry the water to the barrels and then ring the bell so that the cage could be brought back to the surface. It took a lot of water to cook for 100 people, besides washing. Also, the men had to have water to wash with after their day's work.

My parents had a African-American yard man who refused to go down in the mine to fill the barrels. He said, "I never get in a hole that I can not see out of." So, my mother would go down in the mine, fill the barrels, and ring to have them hoisted to the surface. She said she had a yoke across her shoulders with a bucket on each side. She would go to the place where the water was, fill the buckets, carry them to the barrels (which were on the cage) and empty them, until the barrels were full. The African-American, of course, took care of the barrels when they reached the top of the shaft. 117

Sometimes, water gave generously:
We had lots of rain and fast thaws those days and water came down at a great rate and pushed the ice up and over to

the banks like a huge bulldozer. We could pick fish out of the pools along the banks and in the timber. 118

...and beautifully:
She always attempted to watch the ice go out of the river every spring. I don't think it ever failed. I remember her wading through a puddle half-way up to her knees rather than lose time going around to get to the river bank. Once we were awakened in the night by the roar. Lucky it was a clear, full-moon nite. Us kids all piled out and followed. What fun! 119

In times of drought, there was not enough; and then there was too much:
One Sunday morning, everyone in Pierre was down watching the big chunks of ice breaking away in the river, which was assisted, too, with gunpowder. Then the flats in Pierre were beginning to flood. We went back to our hotel but just before twelve o'clock noon, the water had reached the hotel and soon was six feet in the dining room. The afternoon of that day they decided the hotel's two upper stories were overloaded and the immense ice cakes might cause trouble with the building, so all guests were ordered to the hilltops.

Mother took her trunk, too, and we had to go out the second-story windows and down tall ladders. Mother sat up all night, afraid there might be thieves through the night. The next morning the flood had gone down the river and we could go back to our hotel, which we did, but had to pay $25.00 for the trunk and ourselves for transportation. 120

Another event she used to tell about was the tragic flood that took eleven lives on Beaver Creek in June, 1879. A group of freighters were camped on the Creek when a flash flood roared down the valley, sweeping everything before it, including machinery intended for the Homestake.121

They were awakened by a loud roaring at three a.m. Thinking it was the wind, looking out the window, instead of the wind, they saw a wall of water, twelve-feet high, coming down the creek. Before we could get out, the house was half-full of water, moving just across the creek. 122

Mrs. Holly tells of the great flood of early in the century when the creek overflowed and took the pilings away from the bridges. Trains could not cross over the unsafe bridges and, as the creek could not be forded, the people on the north side of town were without food. Mox Paznansky, a well-known pioneer, crossed over the unsafe bridge by walking on the ties of the railroad bridge and brought food for the families living there. 123

Rebecca Ann Thomas Payton Doud and George W. Doud who heard reports on several occasions that the Indians were on the "warpath".

Indians

The crimes of the United States government against the Lakota compounded, one on another. The sacred lands of the Black Hills were taken illegally, and the Indians suddenly were ordered (in violation of the 1868 Ft. Laramie treaty) onto reservations. When instead they gathered, as they had each summer in memory, for the sundance and friendship, they were attacked by the U.S. army at the Little Big Horn. The Lakota defeated the seventh cavalry forces of General George A. Custer, and defended their land:

On several occasions it was reported that the Indians were on the way up Rapid Valley and were on the war path. All the neighbors would then get the women and children together in one house or take them to Rapid City and the men would stay on guard.124

"This young man started out for Beulah, riding a valuable horse. When he saw the Indians, he started to run for Beulah; then he turned toward Spearfish, and the Indians rose up in front of him. The Indians were very careful not to damage the horse."
"They kept closing in until they had him at close quarters and knocked him off his horse. Do you know, that riderless horse bolted right through the Indians and came back to Spearfish! Maybe if the young man had given the horse his head he could have come through all right."
"Rhodes, the father of the two children buried in the cemetery, was killed by Indians after I came. He and some friends went after the Indians to recover some stolen stock, and caught up with them near the Bell Fourche river."
"Rhodes was shot. They rolled him in a blanket and buried him in a shallow grave till they could come back for his body. I remember my father saying one of the Indians in that raiding party was unusually tall." 125

Rumors of Indian atrocities abounded:
One time the Indians stole all their horses and oxen, and some bullwhackers gave our grandfather the two horses they had left to get the family to the fort. My grandmother held

my mother, to keep her from crying so that the Indians would not hear them. Later they heard that these men were all burned at the stake by the Indians.

The Indian reservation was close by and the ranchers had to keep a close watch on their supplies -- else the Indians would steal them. One such incidence, I remember hearing my folks tell about, was the time Mother had just finished papering their two-room log house with leaves from The Breeders Gazette, about the only magazine or paper they did get in those days, if any. They had a "store room" where they kept their bacon, fresh meat, sugar, flour and such things. On this occasion, they had just butchered some pork a day or so before. Mother and my Aunt Jenny were alone at the house when up rode an Indian. He came into the house, looked at the paper on the wall, then pointed to a picture of a pig -- said he wanted some. They told him they had none. He said, "You lie!" Then he went into the store room, helped himself to some sugar, a couple of cured hams, got on his horse and was just about to leave when here came Uncle Sime. He was told about what happened, fired a few shots into the general direction of the Indian. The Indian immediately dropped the hams and sugar and rode away, but fast! 126

Mother said that many times word would come that the Indians were on the war path, and so all the women and children would be taken down into the mine until the scare was over. 127

By 1880, the reports of Indians defending themselves against the intruders stopped. The government's forced relocation policy gradually took hold. Finally, in the winter of 1890, with the government pushing its largest land grab, the major resister to it, Sitting Bull, was killed. His remaining band, and that of Big Foot, fled in terror, heading for sanctuary with Red Cloud at Pine Ridge. Intercepted by the army, almost 300 Lakota refugees, flying the white flag of peace, were massacred at Wounded Knee Creek. Most of them were women and children.

The Black Hills pioneer women only knew that there had been an "Indian uprising." Most of them, it appears, never knew the genocidal nature of the army attack on the

Lakota. **They did know, from their own experience, that these Indians posed no threat to them, and were hungry.**

She returned to Omaha, and came again in [1890]. That was the year of the Indian uprising and she was quite unhappy, afraid to stay and afraid to travel back over the route. She considered her parents had come to the end of the world.128

Also other tribes of Indians visiting from other reservations used this trail. Their campgrounds can still be located by the circle of stones where their tepees were set. They were always ready to trade their baskets, beads and trinkets for coffee, sugar or watermelons. There was always an abundance of melons on Andy's farm in season. But, he experienced no trouble with the Indians.

Even in the perilous times when the uprisings were prevalent, in the summer of 1889, it was reported to this little colony of settlers, that the Indians were preparing for war. They immediately loaded their covered wagons with groceries and taking women and children, started for Crawford, Nebraska, to be near the fort and soldiers, some of the men remaining at home to care for the stock.

The next year during the winter of 1890, there was a great discontent among the Indians on both the Rosebud and Pine Ridge reservations leading on to the battle of Wounded Knee in December. The alarm was again sent out to the settlers. Families moved together for greater protection. Andy and William Landers moved their families together. Both were young men with families of small children. The women were very fond of each other, and the children never quarreled. They spent a happy winter together, even though the men were ever on the watch for unfriendly Indians.129

The tunnel, port-hole trench to provide protection against the Indians was dug on the Leroy Guffey ranch, located near the west line of Meade County and on the north side of the river, across from the mouth of Nine Mile Creek.

No one lives on the place now, but the house still stands. The tunnel caved in years ago. The last time Mrs. Jenks was there, the imprints of the tunnel and every port-hole were still clearly to be seen, even though cattle had tromped over it for years. She does not remember the names of the people who were killed by Indians twenty-five miles east of her father's claim. Nellie was only twelve years old at that time. She knows the place the massacre took place was well-marked for years -- the burned wagon irons remained.

      She also knows that a Lakota woman with a child on her back had been left on the prairies during a storm. This Lakota woman made her way to a white family on Cherry Creek whom she knew. They cared for the refugees until the storm subsided -- then two sons of the family took the Indians back to the reservation by wagon.130

      At the time of the battle of Wounded Knee and Messiah Craze, the men were called to fight the Indians. Not taking the older men, Grandfather Judson was left home to care for the women. Mother, my aunt and the children hid in a cave at the White place, but would venture out once a day to go from house to house to see about the chores. Grandfather would go ahead with a shotgun over his shoulder to protect them against any intruder. In later years, Mother would relate the incident and would laughingly say "I often wondered what we would of done if an Indian had appeared." 131

      The rumor prevailed that the Indians were again on the warpath. One day a large band of Indians showed up at her place. There were fifty wagons of them -- men, women and children. Their vehicles, single file, were stretched along 160 acres. Mrs. Tarrant thought for sure she and her family were going to get scalped.

      A couple of the men came over to her and asked if they could water their horses. "I was really relieved, as you can well imagine," she said. It turned out that the Indians were taking their children to the Indian school at Rapid City... After that the Indians often stopped at Mrs. Tarrant's to water their horses. "Never once did any one of them pick up anything that didn't belong to them. They always paid for what they got." she asserted. 132

      "During the first year [1890] we had an Indian scare. A warning came to us and we were ordered to move. I remember we drove at night in terror for our lives...me with a gun across my lap while my husband drove. The cause of all this was a regiment of Crow Indians who sent scouts on ahead. When the homesteaders saw tracks of moccasined feet, they sent out the alarm. No one was molested and we soon returned to our home." 133

My father had acquired a ranch on the Cheyenne River, and stocked it with cattle. He usually took us all with him when he went on inspection trips, and one of those trips was during the Indian scare. While we were there we saw an Indian coming, and we were so frightened. But all he wanted was food, so mother fed him and he went on. 134

That was in 1890. It was during the Indian scare. Some neighbors came to our house, nights, during the uprising, for protection. Mother had always been shy of guns. During the scare they, Mother and Dad, slept on the floor near the doors. Dad had a good rifle and got mother a good and heavy two-barreled shotgun. She learned to shoot it and had it beside her at night. Fortunately, the scare did not last long. 135

[During] the Indian scare of 1890-91, when ranch families were warned to flee to nearby settlements, "A neighbor rode up one day and told me the Indians were coming and suggested I move into town," Mrs. Woods said. "But I was doing my washing and I told him I couldn't leave. Besides, I had just received a new sewing machine and I wasn't going to leave that for the Indians." 136

Mrs. Della Westover of Fairburn will observe her ninety-third birthday on December 28. Ironically, that's the same date on which the Wounded Knee massacre took place sixty-one years ago. Mrs. Westover was thirty-two-years-old on that infamous day, but she wasn't celebrating her birthday.

"We had heard lots of reports that the Indians were on the warpath," Mrs. Westover remembers. "So we went into the foothills along French Creek and stayed in some cabins which had been abandoned by miners. But the Indians never bothered us. The Wounded Knee incident is one which the white folks can feel ashamed of," the pioneer woman declared.137

"I wasn't very afraid of the Indians," said ninety-year-old Mrs. Catherine Gray, as she talked of the Indian scare of 1890-91. "I think the most of them would have quieted down if they were given food."

The Gray family worked on the Overpeck ranch. This ranch was situated on Spring Creek and the Indians passed through near the house on their way from the reservation to Rapid City.

However, during the Indian scares the people were often alerted to gather in the school house for protection when the word was passed around that bands of Indians were leaving the reservation. Soldiers from Ft. Meade and Ft. Kearney, augmented by the civilian guards, then went to intercept the bands of red men and send them back to the reservation.

"I often thought," says Mrs. Gray, "that the Indians were going on peaceful missions, and that the white people were too easily scared."

"Once," she continued," everybody was rounded up to go to a school house for safety. The Indians, they said, were only five miles away! My husband was with the civilian guards and so I just stayed on the ranch with the children. I remember I was sorting potatoes that day, picking out seed potatoes to plant. When asked by some of the men, who had warned me, what I'd do if the Indians came, I told him that I'd just give the Indians some potatoes. Cook and serve them a hot meal. That would tame them." The red men had come across the Cheyenne River but were quickly sent back.

At another time some wagons stopped in the yard. Mrs. Gray had been warned not to let the Indians in the house under any circumstances. The man came to the door and said, "Child awful cold. Warm him." "The child was nearly frozen," she says, "and so I asked the man to come in. I fried up some eggs, gave the little boy warm milk and the man, coffee. They were so grateful. I asked him where the mother of the boy was and he pointed up and said, 'gone up', I took that to mean she was dead."

At another time a very sad thing happened within sight of the ranch house windows. Mrs. Gray noticed a wagon stopping near the ranch. The Indian man got out and took his gun and, lying flat on his stomach, began to crawl forward. She noticed a rabbit watching him curiously. One shot and the man had the rabbit. He carried it back to the wagon where his wife was sitting on the seat. The man flung the rabbit into the back of the wagon and started to lay the gun in. Something happened and the gun discharged, hitting the woman in the back, killing her instantly.

Such wailing and weeping she had never heard, said Mrs. Gray. "I wanted to go out and see if I could do something to help but others at the ranch warned me to stay in and leave the man alone with his grief."

The man keened and cried for some time. Finally, he wrapped his loved one in a blanket, laid the body on some hay in the wagon and drove away with his sad burden. "I cried for him that day," she reports. 138

She also brought her organ from her home in Iowa and it was a novelty in this country. The Indian Reservation was about five miles away, so the Indians seemed to be always travelling by our place, either to go hunting or fishing. They had a kindly feeling towards the folks as father was their friend. The Indian women liked to hear mother play the organ, it was an instrument of mystery to them. She also sewed for them, and many a calico dress was made by mother for an Indian woman. They were so grateful to her for this, that would bring her gifts of bead work or venison they had killed near our place.

At this time the Indians we knew so well were in a war-like mood, being previous to the Battle of Wounded Knee. So, many Indians were holding meetings near our place. Finally, the neighbors asked for some protection and through the efforts of father and his immediate neighbors, soldiers were sent to our locality from Fort Meade. The neighbors came to our place to be near the protection of the soldiers. Naturally, all this confusion and the uncertainty of the behavior of the Indians was hard on Mother, so as soon as she was able to travel, she left for her home in Iowa with my sister and I. She remained there until this Indian trouble was over. 139

Not one single white person was injured during this time, although the newspapers, for almost six months, had whipped-up the settlers to believe that the Indians were after them. The wonder is not that some white people, who knowingly broke the law and settled on Indian land, were

killed by the defending Lakota. Instead, the wonder is that so few were killed. And the miracle is that the Lakota, like indigenous people from the time of Columbus on, often offered friendship to the invaders.

Their decision to come west to make their permanent home brought them to the Black Hills via wagon train, although they had stopped in Springfield, South Dakota, near an Indian reservation, where he was employed by the government and, while he was engaged in his work, she proceeded to teach Indian children even if it meant bringing them into her own home, which was later enlarged to accommodate all.

As a young bride, she was terrified of the Indians, although their trip west was uneventful in this respect. After their arrival, the Indians did steal their team and saddle horse. In telling me about this, she told me how she was trying to make the first batch of bread she had ever attempted and upon hearing a noise near the door she turned to see three Indian women watching her. She almost froze with fear, but noticing their friendly looks and outstretched hands, she forced herself to smile, beckoning them to come into her kitchen, which they did, and proceeded to teach her how to make bread. From that day until she died, she excelled in her breadmaking. Later, due to this friendly gesture on her part, she and grandfather found their horses had been returned and were tied in the back yard, none the worse for wear. Grandmother taught these Lakota women, and others, many of our ways, including quilt-making. Her children acquired many of the Indian ways by associating and playing with their children. They even learned to speak the Sioux language. 140

"Indian scares were common, but it was more scare than actual hurt. I don't believe my husband was ever really scared of the Indians. When he was away, once in a while I had to tend the post office." 141

Long strings of Indian wagons and horsebackers went by our place. They camped some by Lonewell, which was by our place. We could hear them singing and see them dancing.142

The Indians never bothered. They were afraid of the Black Hills. They said it was the Mount of Evil Spirits.143

Indians were still a source of danger in the country. In later years Mrs. Davis told of one night when she heard the tramp of horse's feet coming nearer and nearer. She lay listening with bated breath, hoping, if it were Indians, they would take their horses and go. Morning revealed the tracks of many horses but those belonging to Davis and Spaulding were still there.

Later it was learned that the riders were moving some horses to another range. This incident is one of many that would have struck terror to a fainter-hearted woman. But Mrs. Davis remained and did her part in the taming of the wild country.144

There were many Indians here at that time. Their trail from the reservation to their hunting ground in Wyoming was about a mile from his home.

"I was afraid the Indians would take our baby, so to satisfy their demands for food, I went to the cellar and got some of Mother's homemade bread and told them to catch some chickens from the farmyard", recalls Mrs. Comes. "They still wanted more 'chicks', but were able to catch only two of the frightened fowl. After the Indians were given food, they left peaceably", she remembers.

She had been left at home to care for her two younger sisters. The episode above occurred in the early spring of 1884, when the Mayer family had moved to Dakota from Waterloo, Iowa, by horse and wagon. Of their several contacts with Indians, this one seems to have left the strongest impression on the mind of the frightened child. 145

On the second day out from Pierre, the outfit was "attacked" by Indians. A bottle of alcohol which one man had brought along because he had heard the water was bad, was the cause of the "attack", as the Indians had whiffed the alcohol!* "There were twelve young Indians in the bunch, and they changed their ideas quickly when they saw me," said Grandma with a twinkle in her eyes.

In fact, there were two young ladies in the wagon train that claimed the Indian's attention, but Grandma more than the other because she was almost a platinum blonde. The other girl, her friend, was a dashing redhead, and the two girls seemed to wield a spell over the young Indians because of their hair. It was strange to them, and they ran their fingers through the silken hair almost as if they could hardly believe what they saw. The two girls cringed in fear and tried hard not to let on, but the Indians harmed no one in the whole outfit. When the wagon train managed to get underway again, the Indians followed. To look back and realize a dozen Indians were trailing them, put terror into the hearts of those early pioneers. They kept going until eleven o'clock that night, the Indians trailing along, whiffing the alcohol aroma and wondering about the two unusual-looking girls.146

... They were sometimes frightened by Indians and tramps but never did them any harm.147

After I Zora was married, she went to live at Rockford, then to Pringle and on to Chilson. Her husband left the railroad for a short time to work at a marble quarry. There they all stayed with her sister and family for a short time.
While living in Chilson, one day she and her sister were busy preparing the noon meal. They heard a commotion outside and looked out the window. They saw a band of Indians with knives and hatchets in their belts coming toward the house. Of course, I Zora thought they had come to kill them. Since it was a very cold day in late January, she hurriedly wrapped her three-week-old baby in a blanket, took her two-year-old daughter by the hand, and, forgetting to put anything on herself, she ran the two miles to the marble quarry as fast as she could, to her husband. He thawed the little girl's feet with snow as they were frozen, borrowed coats for them and returned with them to her sister's home.
The Indians had been friendly, however, and only asked for bread and beans which her sister had given them and they had gone away happy.148

Travel

Travel didn't cease once the pioneers reached the Hills. For some women, it had just begun...

About a year after they were married, they moved to Flint Rock Creek. This again was pioneering, this time in a new cattle and ranch country in the northwestern part of South Dakota, before the land was open to homesteaders. Neighbors were few and far between.

The trip to Belle Fourche, a distance of 125 miles, after groceries, clothing and all supplies, was a three weeks, round trip made only twice a year, in the spring and in the fall, by four horse-wagon teams. 149

Transportation came in for its share of discussion and members [of the Deadwood Round Table Club] recalled the big three-seated, horse-drawn hacks which served the public between Deadwood and Lead. Also remembered was the horse-car line which was in operation between first ward and upper Charles Street and proved to be a favorite pastime with the children who had money to pay for a ride. Nearly all the roads were toll and the common expression was that visitors had to pay to enter town and again to get out of it.

The stagecoaches were stopped every ten miles to change horses and the trip was made with four horses going at a steady pace. But upon the coaches' arrival at the old Half-Way House, six fresh horses with fancy, shiny harnesses and trappings were hitched to the coach in order that it might arrive in the busy mining camp with a grand flourish. 150

"It was in 1880 and we had to come from Sydney, Nebraska, by stage. My husband also had the stage ranch. That meant the stage drivers stopped and turned in their tired horses for fresh models, then went on their way," said Mrs. Boland. The coming of the train meant the stage ranch business was discontinued, of course, as folks used the train altogether." 151

In the winter time my Dad went to town; it was too cold a trip for the rest of us to go. In the summertime we went to Hot

Springs once. We stayed all night and camped down along Fall River.152

She saw the country settle as people came from everywhere to get land and make homes. It was never lonely even though it was twenty-five miles to town and required a whole day to make the trip with horses and buggy.
Mrs. Carter saw the crooked little trails go to good dirt roads, then to better roads so the time of reaching town was pared down; then she saw the coming of automobiles, which boiled the time down to almost nothing. 153

The next day they came to Lead on the hack line pulled by horses...There were no sidewalks then and the roads were mostly trails. They had toll gates at Pluma, Central City and on the Terry Road. They built better roads with the money made from the toll gates. 154

I lived seven years on a stock farm driving, at times, thirty miles to town and to see my parents. There were no cars at that time and the drives took several hours.155

It amused Mrs. Jenks to relate how Bert managed to get the house moved. "He got Hans Sorensen to help. The two young fellows manipulated in some manner to get the house blocked up and under it they placed their two running-gears lengthened out. Then they got the house set down onto the wagons and chained and tied on -- and nailed down, maybe. They each took four horses, hitched them side by side, to pull the load."
Then Nellie laughed heartily, "Their shirts were soaking wet -- both had toiled so, prying, propping and giving what leverage their bodies could in hoisting the house. This was an entirely new venture. If you could have seen the picture they made! Bert framed in the open doorway and Hans framed in the open window. That was the way they drove the eight horses. It did look comical! I was on my horse, watching. You know, even then I rode a side saddle. It was not considered lady-like to ride astride -- not even in those days."

Then Nellie resumed her narration. "Occasionally they stopped to investigate if the log chains and every little thing was holding together. That gave the horses time for a breather."

"Their greatest worry was the ominous clouds piling up and rolling about like fury in the west. Just so it held off and brought no rain here. It was an extremely hot day -- so hot it made one's eyes fairly smart, exactly the kind of heat for a sudden cloud-burst."

"But all went well. Horses and house and fellows arrived at the river bank just as it was time for Bert to beat it home to help milk the seventeen cows."

"They unhitched, remarking how fortunate it was the Oliver Rose crossing had such gradual slopes on both sides and the river was practically dry. It would be no shucks at all to cross the river in the morning and, maybe by noon, the house would be down on its new foundation."

"In excellent spirits at having accomplished so much -- the two fellows started to meet here at an early hour next morning. I beat it to bring home the cows, which I loved to do."

"Next day dawned as beautifully as any house-movers could wish, but it promised to be another scorcher -- of this Bert and Hans felt certain as they jogged along on their way home with their teams. Hans was a bachelor, living a good half-mile north of the Barnes' place. Both men were elated because tomorrow would see the completion of this undertaking."

"Next morning to their utter amazement as they approached the river they could hear its roar! Hurrying forward, they saw the rushing waters! The river was almost bank-full!"

Mrs. Jenks said it was a good week before the men calculated the banks were dry enough for them to tackle the job. And during that week, I suppose, Hans found as many uses for his wagon as Bert did -- and there they were, pinned down with the weight of our house on them! But, at last, they had the house moved. Very soon we were settled in our own cozy little home. The next year we added one room and a little porch.156

Travelling in those days was much different. Hilda baked a cake to take to a dance at a neighboring place and upon arriving at the destination in the lumber wagon she discovered it was only crumbs. When they crossed a draw in the sled one winter the sled tipped so much Hilda and baby

Pearl fell out. Pearl, well-bundled, was nearly lost in the snow. The lumber wagon, buggy and sled gave way to the Model T. Theirs was very new and the Hett family were going to town, Bud and Hilda were riding in the back seat with Pearl in front. Hilda disciplined Bud with a sharp spank and Pearl shouted "Daddy we had a blow out." Whereupon Hilda replied, "We did, and we'll have another if this kid doesn't settle down."[157]

Adversity and Overcoming

Some were dealt a tough hand early in life; others faced situational or long-term hardship once they got to the Hills. Remarkably, they carried on with grace, matter-of-fact courage, and even humor.

With the hardships of this time, the pioneer women had a big hand in developing a new country. It has been said that men get the credit for carving a state out of the wilderness, but their plucky, resourceful wives were the ones who made it a fit place to live in. 158

One time my mother and some of the other ladies in the camp were picking service berries. My mother was picking away when she heard a slight rustle on the other side of some trees where she was picking. She thought it was one of the ladies in the group. She talked but did not get an answer. Upon making an investigation, it proved to be a bear. Of course, Mother wasted no time in leaving. She went and joined her other friends. As they were going home, they met one of the men from the camp. He said someone had told him there was a bear in the vicinity, and that he was out to get it, which he did. 159

Her father brought home a cake of something her mother thought was scouring soap, but after trying it on her pots and pans without any success, she learned it was a cake of maple sugar. 160

During that time I was my dad's only helper, for I learned to walk, not cry like some babies. It wasn't very convenient, to hold up my long white dresses, but I got along till one day a good neighbor brought a whole bolt of pink calico and he told mother to fix me out with that. 161

One night the cows didn't come in to be milked. What do you think Dad found next morning early when he went for them? They were huddled around a wee antelope whose mother had been shot. Dad brought it in his arms, all cold. Mother let it have some warm nurses with me and it revived soon, and grew fast, and learned to pick peas and beans before anyone could get to them. 162

There were many small events of interest in those pioneer days. Some humorous ones were the time our neighbor's cow came and ate up all of mother's yeast which was spread on a table to dry. Another time the same cow ate most of the soap which was put out to harden. Also when that same neighbor's home burned down and someone sympathized with her, she remarked that there probably wasn't any other way to get rid of those bedbugs. It was a log house. 163

When I was seven the Hulst and Price Lumber Company in Rapid City was looking for a superintendent for their timber operation at Nemo. They persuaded father to sell them his mill, and take the job. Mother and father then moved to Nemo, leaving us children in Rockerville to continue school.

In November my nine-year-old sister and I both contracted a bad type of whooping cough, and had to stay out of school. So mother came after us one day and expected to get home by the next day. She had a fast team and light buggy and could very well make it in one day if all went well.

We started early, but coming down Spring Creek Hill, which was then almost continuous rock for a long stretch, an extra bad jolt jerked the tongue out of the neck yoke and it fell against a ledge and splintered right between the horses. With nothing to hold it, it slammed from side to side against one and then the other horse and away they went down that hill.

My sister and I were scared to death and tried to jump out. But mother knew that might be fatal, so she had to hold us in while she tried to control the team. They were frantic and tried desperately to get away from that flailing tongue. Just as we reached the bottom of the hill, she lost one rein and we began to go around in circles.

Fortunately for us the Reeds lived near the road, and Bryce, their son, who was doing the morning chores, saw -- and probably heard -- us. He ran and caught the horses before they upset us.

Mrs. Reed, understandably, did not want her children exposed to the whooping cough, so we sat in the buggy while Bryce got a team and wagon. He tied mother's team behind the buggy, and the buggy to the wagon. Then we started for Rapid City to get a new tongue put in the buggy. We had started early, but by the time the buggy was repaired it was noon. We hurriedly ate a quick lunch and started on, for mother knew father would worry if we didn't get home.

The days were so short that by the time we were only half-way home, the night was impenetrably black, so she stopped at a ranch and they were happy to have us stay through the night. Father met us quite early the next day, and we got home without further incident. 164

A blizzard was brewing one wintry morning, and he went to the barn to check the condition of the stock. The barn doors blew open and struck him across the face, causing a blood clot in his one good eye. For three days, they were marooned on the farm. When he could get to town to have his eye examined, it was too late. The sight was gone.

Blinded, a wife and two small children in his responsibility, a farm to run -- Dick Johnson made up his mind to learn to live without sight. He dug irrigation ditches, gardened, learned to do everything that was needed by feel and determination. He still prides himself on being the one to keep the woodbox filled in their home back in Roubaix, and walks around with the ease of a man who sees exactly where he is going.

One of his jokes concerns the time he took a friend down in the potato cellar to show him some of his prize potatoes. After stumbling around a bit, the friend embarrassedly admitted to Dick that the cellar was pitch dark, and that he couldn't even see the potatoes. 165

It is hard to tell my mother's story. She is so missed. The facts of her life cannot convey, to one who did not know her, such personality and worth.

Ena Cassels was born in Swan County, Indiana, January 1st, 1864. She lost her eye-sight in an accident when she was nine years old and received most of her education at the Iowa School for the Blind in Vinton. The family came to the Black Hills during her last year at school, so she came by rail to Pierre and then on by stagecoach.

Her father, George Cassels, had come from Scotland when fourteen, and was a versatile, progressive man. He pioneered in Colorado and the Black Hills, building and operating one of the first stamp mills, the Cassel Mill at Central City, and had extensive mining interests. Her mother was of Pennsylvania Dutch descent, kind and sensible.

The Cassel family lived in a ranch house between Vale and Empire, and having five young people at home, was the center of social life. People drove long distances and stayed to visit. Sunday dinners and singing bees brought people together. Ena organized the "Literary Society," which met in a school house. She helped with Sunday School and played the organ. Boys riding to the Hills brought the new songs and read the music to her.

Among all the friendly voices, she liked that of young Will Lancaster. Will had driven a four-mule team through from Missouri in the early part of 1880, had brought freight wagons from Pierre on a hazardous trip, and was hunting buffalo. They walked to the post office on summer evenings and Will picked for her the first wild roses. She liked him a lot.

Will took a homestead and built his house of logs on the north side of the Belle Fourche River, near the Bismarck Crossing. Will and Ena were married August 30, 1886. That first fall, Ena went in the wagon with Will, staying alone at their camps while he rode horseback, hunting.

They started the winter of 1887 with a fine herd of young cattle but had few left after the storms of that terrible winter. Farming alone in the ensuing dry years did not pay.

I was born at Empire in January of 1889. After spending a few months in Central City we moved to Hot Springs, then a boom town. There, in 1891, my sister, Mary Hazel, was born. Mother took care of her children, cooked, washed, ironed, cleaned and sewed.

Her health was poor for a long time. A trip to California did not help but outdoor life in a mining camp at Mystic made her cross or impatient. At Mystic, she ordered Sunday School papers, beads to string and kindergarten cards to sew. She spent time with us picking berries, and roaming the hills. She sang to us, and taught, and amused us.

Later we moved to Gayville, and I entered school in the second grade. Dad's prospecting finally found a good claim, which he sold. He then gave up mining for a little store at the end of the railroad, Belle Fourche. On a lovely day in June, 1898, we drove down in a buggy behind old Fanny. We were in business there until 1946.

The store saw good times and bad. Mother always knew next year would be better. Husband and children were secure in her understanding and sympathy.

She liked people and had a kindly appreciation of their strength and weakness. She was a tireless worker for causes she believed in. She taught Sunday School, played the organ and encouraged pastors and school teachers. When church money was raised the hard way, she canvassed the town and countryside. She made countless chicken pies and nut cakes for church suppers and always helped town betterment.

William Hugh Jr. was born in 1902 and soon our house and yard was over-run with noisy small boys and their pets. She read to the children and made them taffy and popcorn balls.

We young folks all attended college although times were hard those years. She wrote us wonderful letters.

Mother used her many braille books and enjoyed the braille magazines when they became available. Almost as much as Dad, she enjoyed riding to the Hills. At first we used the team, then a big, old Overland which she nick-named "Emmer" for the emergencies always arising when on the road.166

They were blessed with fifteen children, four who died in infancy, in my grandmother's arms, of whooping cough and diphtheria. My grandfather made their tiny caskets which my grandmother tenderly lined with sheets. They buried their babies on the ranch with their own simple rites.

Churches were scarce in those days, as were undertakers' services. My grandfather then decided to make cabinets, at which he excelled, using the beautiful pines which were so plentiful. He also made caskets for his neighbors and friends, as needed.167

Blizzards, Cyclones and Fires

A major topic of conversation at the time as well as in later remembrances, the weather defined the nature of existence. Tornadoes (called cyclones then) destroyed quickly and often without warning. While the path of a cyclone seldom cut a wide swath, blizzards settled over the entire region, and more than once a season.

She was in Lead when a cyclone struck, causing the boxcars to fly off the track. 168

As we had no team and wagon, my father hired a Deadwood man to haul a load of provisions for the winter. The snow was so deep and heavily-crusted that it was impossible for him to break through to the ranch. Leaving everything stuck, he walked to our house. The next day, the men made a large hand sled and put it on long skis. With this they brought the stranded supplies in by manpower. Since one of the men became snow-blind, they had to put him on the sled to bring him home. The teamster started back the next day and camped that night near Beulah. During the night his wagon caught fire from his big campfire. He lost the wagon and everything he had with him. 169

Farming was not very profitable at this time, making it necessary for Mr. Wallace to work away from home a great deal of the time. He helped to build the railroad when it was being built from Crawford to Edgemont. During the winter of 1894, while he was working away from home, there came a terrible snowstorm. The drifts were so deep it was impossible to get the cow or horse out of the barn. Mrs. Wallace had to melt snow for water for the animals to drink. She was alone with the small children for several days until Mr. Wallace could get home. 170

In the terrible blizzard of 1910 Carter lost his way one night when he was coming home, or his saddle horse may have kicked him. He was found dead at the door of their daughter's home while the daughter was with her mother.

"His coffin had to be made of boards, and they made a rough-box too, and he was buried on our own land," said Mrs.

Carter. She stayed with their claim and made final proof on the land after her husband's death. 171

In 1887, Rebecca Anne came from California to visit her mother and brothers. One day in January of that year, Mrs. Stevens and Rebecca started home from what is known as the Somervold ranch on the bench east of the site of Minnesela, a two mile walk. They had spent the day assisting in some work at the house. They were caught in a raging blizzard, one of those storms in which the wind seems to come from all directions, swirling around the luckless person caught out in it. Fine snow blinds the eyes as the wind just about takes the breath. The two women spent most of the night walking in a circle (as was shown by their tracks), then finally found a shack on the edge of the Crooked Oak country in which they took refuge. They were found there by a searching party called out to look for them.172

In September of the year 1879, when the town of Deadwood was almost totally destroyed by fire, Mrs. Colman and a little son, who was only a few days old, had to be removed from their home, which was in the path of the fire. Home and business were wiped out in this fire, and once again, in 1894, the family was to lose both home and business in a destructive fire. 173

The abundance of timber provided building material lacking on the treeless prairies. But there was a price to be paid for this richness, as the white settlers soon learned.

"When we were on our claim, fire was a constant danger then, just like it is now, here in the Black Hills. One time five freight wagons camped thirty-five miles from our land.
"They dug holes and built camp fires to cook supper and breakfast, but they were short of water so couldn't douse their fire. They did try, though, and covered it over with dirt. A ninety-mile-an-hour wind whipped up and blew the dirt away. That started one of the most horrible fires known in the country. It spread until it was 125 miles long and sixty miles wide."
"Lots of stock was lost in the fire and it swept right through our homestead. I recall that we brought our horse up to

the door, prepared to take him inside in order to save him. We were lucky as our house was of sod and was on a creek bank. They managed to save it by dipping water from the creek. Men fought the fire with wet gunny sacks. My daughter and her husband lost all the lumber they had hauled out for their new house." 174

The prairie fire that swooped down the draw one hot day in August tested Mother's pioneer courage and strength of character as she stood with the men from the neighboring ranches as the fireguard, hastily burned around the house and barn, with a wet gunny sack to beat out any truant flame that jumped the guard and threatened her home and children.175

They were living in Central at the time of the fire in Deadwood in 1879 and Mrs. Parker recalls hearing about it at the store when she went on an errand. She ran back and told her father who saddled a horse and rushed to Deadwood. Many Deadwood persons stayed at Central City until their homes were rebuilt, she said.176

Social Life

Country or town: where you lived determined what you did for fun.

Our playmates were baby chicks, geese, ducks, calves, colts, and plenty of kittens. Of course, there was always a faithful dog. The boys had four wheels, and they used to make wagons just like Dad's, and since I was the youngest, I could ride, and they were the frisky horses. Many a time I was dumped out. We never went much as the neighbors were few and far between, and we were contented with our home life on this farm.177

Considered "high elegance" of the day were the dances and social functions of the [Deadwood] Olympic Club staged on the third floor of the Phoenix Block.178

"We had just as good times then as the youngsters do now, too, perhaps better", she added. "The boys and girls of the neighborhood would get together at our house and join us for an evening of singing. My oldest sister played the piano. I sang soprano and my younger sister sang alto. All the others joined in and how we made the rafters ring! Our favorites were 'Darling Nellie Gray', 'Seeing Nellie Home' and 'The Sweet Bye and Bye'". They had the first piano in Central City. Her sister had learned to play on the organ in the Methodist church, though, before they had their piano.

Hayrack rides and the sleigh rides were fun, too. Sometimes the young people would stop at the dance hall which was at the foot of the hill. Or they might just drive around awhile, then go to one of their homes and fix something to eat."

Picnics and berry-picking were a favorite pastime in those days. The favorite picnic ground was at Woodville about six miles from Central. One fourth of July it snowed, and they had a snowball fight right in the summertime. 179

She was the only woman for miles around who had a sewing machine, so her first visitors were women who came to make their baby clothes at our place. These sewing affairs helped in other ways than getting the children clad; they had fun, too. 180

Amusement was not overlooked in those days, and the young folks in Central City used to get up home talent plays and masquerade dances that brought people from everywhere. Sometimes they would sell as high as 500 tickets to a dance, and the town once had an Independence Day celebration that went over big. 181

Phantom Balls were very popular at this period. Picnicking in the summer and sleighriding in the winter gave Mrs. Monismith many happy hours. 182

Anna and Eva Jackson attended school in the building now known as Lincoln Hall, which was erected in 1884. "Lincoln Hall," she remembers, "was intended for a community center and was used at various times for a literary and debating society's meetings, a dance hall, a roller skating rink and a Catholic Church."

"Times were different then. We enjoyed ourselves more. Everybody was friendly. Matt Bingham, who played for dances, could make his fiddle almost talk. The cowboys loved to dance and they came from miles around to help make, and to share, the fun."183

"Our nearest neighbor in those early years was two miles away...bachelors living there to winter cattle. Our nearest woman neighbor was nine miles away," Mrs. Ernest says. 184

In those days people went to different people's houses and had dances. Later on they had what they called Harvest Festivals and Rodeos and dances.185

Mrs. Cushing was the only woman in this part of the county when Mrs. Davis came. Mrs. Davis visited her on July 4th and she returned the visit in September. 186

Mother was a great entertainer and loved to go. She took us to church and Sunday School every Sunday, weather permitting, often loading her organ in back of buggy or wagon, to play at private funerals, or even dances in private homes.

Mother was an accomplished horsewoman. Travelling to Sturgis or Belle Fourche, loaded with four to seven kids, to a fourth of July celebration, meant nothing to her. Community picnics were a big event.

She saw to it that Christmas and Easter were fully celebrated, making us all new dresses and shirts for the occasion, even to new shoes, if at all possible.187

The people of the Dry Creek community sponsored dances at the Stone schoolhouse, providing refreshments and music by local talents. The dances were always well-conducted and continued to grow in popularity. No liquor was allowed. All had wonderfully good times at these dances. Chris frequently played his violin. The Scandinavians in our community did a lot of visiting and had many parties, especially in winter.188

For recreation they went to dances at Jacob's saloon. Road shows were more recreation. They were given in the old Miners Union Building. 189

"All the young folks liked to ride horseback. That was more fun when a bunch of us went riding. But, best of all, I loved to dance. My family never seemed to care to learn to play cards -- and mother disapproved of card playing."

"In the winter there was many a taffy-pull, or popcorn party at one place or another. One evening, in our little two-room shack, several met to pop corn. We made a bushelbasket full of balls. Next evening we went to another home and did the same -- and so on -- till we had enough corn, great big balls, for the Thanksgiving program at Vale. Here the admission was ten cents. The funds were to be used to buy candy and nuts for treats at the Christmas tree program."

"People came from far away: Andrew Erickson from Horse Creek, Sanford Summers from Whitewood Creek, and from the west, and from east of Empire as far away as ten miles."

"My sister Sadie and Bee Glover and Hazel Jenks often came and all three stayed a week at our house. The girls gladly did all the work if only I would sew dresses for them to wear to the dances. We had lots of fun. Their boyfriends dropped in for the evenings and we danced."

"What music did you have?"

Nellie smiled whimsically, "The world's best! On our small Edison, cylindrical phonograph. We still have it. It plays as good as ever. How our grandchildren love it now!"190

"Those were our barns -- see -- and the dances we used to give there, my, -- everybody had a good time. For one dance we gave, I roasted seven turkeys, young ones they were, and we raised them. I baked fourteen cakes for that dance."

"We never danced on Saturday night," she explained. "We always had our dances on Friday nights, because we never quit until daylight and many a time the crowd had breakfast before they left for home."

"We went miles and miles to a dance -- in wintertime we used a sled, or sleigh, and in other seasons a wagon or buggy," she explained. Mrs. Miller still loves to go to the old-time dances and her only lament is that, because of a weak heart, her husband has to forego that pleasure.

"Do you know how we managed to keep our feet warm in winter when we went to a dance miles away?" she wanted to know. "We'd heat a big rock, wrap it up and put it at our feet and it kept us warm for hours."

"Yes, and do you remember that mean trick you and the rest played on me one time with the thermometer?" chimed in Miller, laughing. The two long-time married folks seem always to have little jokes they like to talk over and laugh about, even yet. Mrs. Miller did remember, vividly.

"It was too cold to go to a dance, my husband said. Well, when he went out to do the chores we brought the thermometer in and warmed it up. Naturally, when he looked at it later, he admitted the weather had warmed considerably -- we went to the dance all right," she said, laughing. I'd 'a froze sure enough if I'd known how cold it really was," said Miller, "but they told me afterwards about cooking the thermometer."

When the Miller cabin was finished, with Mrs. Miller doing the chinking herself, they held a big dance, the favorite form of entertainment. 191

The women formed clubs immediately and stayed with them throughout their lives, doing community service, expanding their minds, and enjoying each others' company:

It was begun by a little group of women in a pioneer mining town on the fringe of the wilderness, who felt a crying need for culture. Starting as a purely social group, their meeting took place at the home of Mrs. Smead; they all brought their sewing, and the conversation was principally concerned with, "how a luncheon should be served." 192

During the last twenty years on the ranch, mother took an active part in the woman's club that had been organized and federated in the 1920's. They sponsored a Sunday School, Extension Club, 4-H Club, and also helped needy families and furnished a room at the original Belle Fourche hospital. To do all this, they raised money by furnishing food and serving suppers at dances at the community hall. She personally took charge of the sale of TB Christmas seals.

The club sponsored a community Christmas tree, and she always saw to it that children who were not able to attend, received the usual bag of candy and nuts. To help raise money for the club she collected recipes from all the pioneer women and printed them with a hand press and made a recipe cabinet. This project cleared $50.00 which was a considerable amount during the depression days. 193

My father came from Canada to Deadwood in 1876. My mother, sister and I followed in May, 1877. Later on, I went away to school in the East, returning after three years. I have been active in the church, club and social life of Deadwood all these past years, being a member of the Episcopal Church and a charter member of the Thursday Club which was organized in 1895. In 1889 I was married to Robert N. Ogden, a young and prominent attorney.194

I'm still going strong at eighty-two years of age in spite of having suffered a broken arm this last winter. Except for three years in which I was travelling around the world and spending some time in Sumatra and Java, I have kept an active interest in Club work.195

Mrs. Haxby was instrumental in having the oldest house in Rapid City (at the present time) reconditioned. The cabin now stands in Halley park. The late Charles Buell had bought the property where the cabin stood originally. Mrs. Haxby and the late Mrs. Alice Gossage, pioneer newspaper woman, appealed to the Fortnightly Women's club to take over the project of having it moved to Halley park and reconditioned. The club raised $300.00 and the Lions club voluntarily donated $25.00 for the additional expenses. At the time of the removal of the cabin, Mrs. Haxby entered a contest conducted by the <u>Household</u> magazine, offering prizes for the two best articles on civic projects. The local woman was winner of the second prize of $50.00, which was used in the maintenance of the building.196

I was one of the founders of the Woman's Literary Club of Sturgis in 1913, and a charter member of Sturgis Woman's club; belonged to that organization for 60 years. 197

She was a charter member of the Lead Woman's Club, and they loved and honored her, all through the years, depending on her for council and advice, for she remained active in the club until she was past eighty.198

Marriage

Courtship and marriage took on a distinct regional flavor.

Lillie was married to John T. Ayer, who had come to the Black Hills from Plymouth, Massachusetts in 1878. They eloped and were married at Central City by Reverend Phifer of the Congregational Church. We used to ask her who was at her wedding, and she always laughed, and said, "The minister and his wife and a little yellow dog." We have a piece of her wedding dress, a beautiful blue taffeta-like material. 199

She recalled her wedding dress as she sat sewing on a patchwork quilt. "It was of wine-colored silk and trimmed in a darker wine-colored satin," she said.
"It was made with a polonaise overskirt. It was very pretty and fitted me so nicely. My husband gave me a pair of matching bracelets that I have yet. They were gold with real ruby sets. I wore them at my wedding but never wore but one at a time after that." She keeps them now in a safety deposit box. She says they are her most cherished possession. 200

Mrs. Rail enjoyed working at the boarding house, teasing the Chinese cook and going dancing with the young men at Deadwood and Central City. The waltz, schottisch, and quadrilles were popular in those days. She met Joe Rail, an "amalgamator"* for the Homestake, at a dance in Central City. After a short courtship, they were married, Father Welch officiating. She was seventeen at the time. The Rails had eleven children. 201

While the men built on some land near Hot Springs, Mattie Dennis kept house for her father and family. It was at this time that the young lady, who could turn out ten loaves of bread a day and make bread pudding minus a material except bread, met young George A. Turner who built the first cabin there and was interested in cattle -- and in girls!
"He was sitting on a log when I first saw him and it was love at first sight. He was a graduate of Boyle's Business

College. There were plenty of nice cowboys around," laughed Mrs. Turner.

The situation was as complicated as a modern, western, fiction yarn. Mattie was engaged to another young man and Turner was also engaged to another young lady, so it looked hopeless.

Deadwood beauties got to coming to Hot Springs all decked out in evening gowns, with trains so long they had to be carried on the arm when the girls walked. This built up some competition, in a way, but the Dennis girls had a sewing machine, so they created dresses patterned after the dresses the Deadwood beauties wore. For some reason, Turner liked to appear indifferent to girls at the local dances.

One day, some cowboys asked him to bring the Dennis girls to a dance. Mrs. Turner remembers that with a chuckle. "The snow was a foot deep when George arrived in his lumber wagon to take us to the dance. He acted stand-offish, so I sat just as far away as I could without falling off the wagon seat," said Mrs. Turner with the merriest twinkle in her eyes. Of course, she wore her fancy, long-trained dress and danced until three a.m., although Turner didn't even dance! She was asked to sing and readily complied, singing the only two songs she ever knew.

Mrs. Turner, who is still an attractive woman, must have been quite a belle in those days. She broke her engagement and soon became engaged to another young man, while all this time Turner was, as she puts it, "just kind of hanging around."

One day Turner surprised her by proposing to her and wound up with "I'll give you sixty days." She was already so in love with him that all the time she needed was long enough to make her wedding clothes.

Their wedding was the first important social event in the town as well as the first Hot Springs wedding. Mrs. Turner brought out a yellowed, old slip of paper, that has been lovingly repaired to make it hold together. "Our marriage certificate is dated March 31, 1881, in Dakota Territory. The Justice of the Peace rode horseback thirty-five miles from Custer to marry us. He had no printed blanks so he just wrote it out on a scrap of paper and let it go at that," Mrs. Turner said softly.

The young bride was flanked by two acres of land. Her father had given her the land, and Turner moved a cabin onto the land so the two began housekeeping. 202

"During the summer I always helped Mother in the sawmill boarding house. One day a couple of men came in late to supper and I waited on them. One of them said 'Pretty nice little girl. Wish she was older.' I thought he had a pretty good opinion of himself. But it turned out he must have been all right. That was Gus, and a year later we were married."

The young couple's first home was a sawmill house. Then Gus purchased a homesteader's relinquishment on land adjacent to her father's with a part-frame and part-log house. The young couple prospered and accumulated cattle and horses. Gus soon bought two other farms and the Carlsons still have the three farms which adjoin. 203

A young gentleman by the name of Frank Waugh used to ride a bicycle along with a group of other cyclists to Hill City, from their homes on Spring Creek, near Rockerville, and it was on one of these adventures he met, and became acquainted with, Lillian Hagerman. They were married in Hill City, June 7, 1897, Lillian being twenty-one years of age.204

"The band mentioned was started before our marriage. When we were married, it was twelve below zero. The next day, the band came to serenade the bride, and their horns froze. They made the awfullest noise in trying to play, and finally had to give it up. I invited them in and gave them coffee." 205

Catherine and George Arbuckle

Catherine Maud Boland Arbuckle
Pennington County
1879

A very sad incident happened shortly after their arrival that very much impressed my mother and also impressed me when she told me. A group of immigrants had camped for the night near the creek. It had been raining for two or three days, so local people warned them to camp on higher ground, but they did not heed the warning, and during the night they were drowned by the rising water. It was my Grandmother Boland's first experience in giving a helping hand in those pioneer times. She continued the practice throughout her life and passed the same capability on to my mother, who was able to come to the aid of her neighbors in time of sickness and death.

The family lived at Buffalo Gap a year, then moved to Rapid City where they lived for many years. They moved from Rapid City to a farm west of town in 1884, and it was here that mother grew to womanhood. Life on a farm was hard work and a little dull for a high-spirited redhead and she was thrilled with a chance to take care of the children of the proprietor of the Harney Hotel. The highlight of the day was when the stage would come in from Deadwood, and they would watch to see who was on it. She was having a very exciting time and enjoying herself when a friend of her father told him it was "no place" for a girl of her age. So, much to her disappointment, she had to go back to the farm.

She attended Spearfish Normal (Black Hills Teachers College) for a term and then taught four or five terms of country school. She often told of the poor. However, many of the families stayed through the hard times and became well-to-do. The last term of school was taught in a Swedish settlement at Black Hawk, and most of the children could not speak English, so she used a Montgomery Ward catalog to teach them the English words. She seemed to have a soft spot in her heart for this particular school and enjoyed meeting those former pupils when they were older. She often laughed about the two Ole Olesons in school, and how she told them apart by remembering one had a sister. It was while teaching the school in Black Hawk that she met my father, George L. Arbuckle, whose parents had arrived in Dakota Territory in 1877 and settled in Rapid City.

Soon after teaching at Black Hawk, she moved to Belle Fourche, and managed a dry goods store for her father. While in Belle Fourche she experienced many incidents of a pioneer town; at that time, the largest cattle shipping point in the world. She saw the cowboys come into town, and saw the great herds of cattle arriving at the stock yards. But the most thrilling incident was seeing the Butte County bank being robbed. She had a gun in her store and at the height of the excitement she ran down the street and gave it to a stranger, to help capture the robbers.

Meanwhile, my father was punching cows in South Dakota and Wyoming. He was offered a job as foreman on the Western Ranches, Limited (VVV) ranch on the Little Missouri River, near Alzada, Montana. He took the job, and they were married December 1, 1897, in Deadwood, and went directly to the ranch where they worked for the VVV until 1903. They then homesteaded this place and through the years built it into a large ranch.

When they first moved to Montana, mother did the cooking for the cowboys in the spring, while they were at the ranch gathering horses to be used during the summer and fall roundup. Each fall, the horses were turned out on the range until needed the next spring.

They fed all the people who stopped at the ranch, and the company paid them for the meals. This money was put away in a savings account to be used later to help buy cattle when they started their own ranch. During the summer dad was away on roundups, and mother stayed on the ranch. There was always a man there to ride on a bunch of horses left at the ranch, so she wasn't without help; still, they were lonely times for her. Neighbors were ten or fifteen miles away but they helped out in time of need. She always had a team to drive and would visit the neighbors. Whenever she stopped at a gate she put my brother and I out, opened the gate, led the team through, then put us back in the buggy, for she was afraid the horses might run away with us in there alone. There were dances to attend also, but, since she never danced, she spent the evenings visiting.

The Indians traveled from reservations in South Dakota to those in Montana, and one route was by the ranch. They generally camped on the river near by. They were a source of worry to her. She didn't know how to talk or deal with them and most of the early days she was afraid of them. Although there were no uprisings then, only peaceful migrations, it hadn't been too long since there had been battles and massacres. They stopped at the house when I was only a day or two old and an old Lakota woman insisted on rocking me. Mother was afraid that she might steal me, and breathed easier when the lady caring for us made the Indians leave. They were always begging for food and she would give them anything they asked for, to get rid of them. Dad often teased her and said they probably called her the "Woman They Could Work".

In later years, a group camped near by and let it be known they had a sick baby, so mother went to the camp to see what she could do. She found the baby had a severe cold, so made a syrup from some onions the Indians had. This medicine seemed to help the child and when they left, they gave mother the onions so she would have them in case her own children got sick. Thus, the fear of Indians was gone, and she always visited with them whenever they came by.

There were eight of us children, all born at the ranch, and only neighbor ladies attended mother at our births. When I was born, my Grandmother Boland and my uncle (then six), drove the 100 miles from Rapid City with a horse and buggy. She made the trip without incident until the last day, when dark overtook her and she had to sleep out on the prairie on a chilly October night. When morning came, she found she was near a house and was able to get breakfast before going on. Whenever I make that trip now, I think of the courage and determination she must have had to make that trip alone by buggy in 1898.

It seems we were very fortunate as far as sickness and accidents were concerned. The youngest son died as an infant from a heart condition that possibly could have been corrected now, but the rest of us were always in good health. We had grippe a time or two and the whole family was down in bed, but we managed to get along. Mother used home remedies like the other pioneer women. Her jug of sheep dip was a joke with the family and neighbors. It was used as a disinfectant for everything and mixed with lard to make a salve. Of course it was used as a disinfectant for the livestock, also.

I can remember only a few bad accidents. Once I was badly cut with the old, v-shaped barbed wire, one younger brother was kicked in the head by a horse, and another brother was burned quite badly on one hand, but we never had a doctor come to the ranch except to set my dad's leg when a horse kicked him and broke it.

One Easter Sunday while mother was dyeing eggs (and we were all interested in that), our brother John followed dad when he left to ride. No one missed him until dad returned, then there was a wild dash to look for him. They feared the worst and looked in the creek and water barrel, but found no trace. Finally dad took his horse and found John's tracks in the dust, and found him and two pet cats about two miles from home. He ran away again, and a neighbor brought him home. Aside from these minor troubles we were fortunate and the only tragedy was when our oldest brother was drowned. It was a hard blow to both my mother and dad.

They worked for the VVV until 1903 when the broken leg kept dad from going on the annual roundup, so he decided it was a good time to start out for himself, and it was then that mother's savings account was used. How proud they were when their first cattle were driven home! I was six at the time and remember the big event.

Trips to Belle Fourche, our nearest railroad (fifty miles away), were made each spring and fall. Enough groceries were laid in to last until the next trip. These were staple foods, like bacon, dried fruit, rice, beans, flour and sugar, lard, coffee, etc. Tomatoes were about the only canned food we used. We had pork and beef, chickens, fish, wild game and a large garden. Mother was able to get to town occasionally while she had just two youngsters but as her family increased, trips became less frequent, until she didn't go at all until we got our first car in 1913.

The usual inconveniences that were part of pioneer life, such as having to carry water, and fighting flies and mosquitos, were met without complaint. It was a constant battle to keep the flies out of the house. All we had to kill them with was sticky and poison flypaper, so we would use willow branches to chase them out of the house and then try to keep the house dark. A smudge was built by the house the keep the mosquitoes away.

The problem of getting us older children to school was a worry. I did not go until I was eight and enough children were available to have a school nearby. The teacher stayed at the school with us smaller children, took care of us and cooked and taught, too. We walked some of the time, four miles, and our biggest worry was that the range cattle would chase us. Later we attended school in Spearfish for a year and then returned to the country school as we were old enough to ride horseback. It was a constant worry, for fear we would be lost in a storm while walking or riding the four or five miles to school.

In 1916 we moved to Spearfish, and the folks bought a house there so my older brother and I could go to the Normal and the others to grade school. We lived there four years and then moved back to the ranch.206

Ellen Boyce Bryant
Lawrence County
1877

    With eggs at five cents a dozen, milk at five cents a quart, and even a good, fat hen for a quarter, the Boyce purse expanded. Money has roots and the Boyce's knew how to tend it. But, they are a part of the grasshopper story. The voracious insects did dastardly damage. Father Boyce had dug trenches. Into these each member, armed with a switch or sack, chased the marauders into the opening where a kerosene bath, warm with a match, made a real inferno.
    The promise of a great new crop of these menaces was evident. Eggs were deposited by fence posts, stumps, decayed wood -- every place. The sun was darkened by oncoming hordes. An oil cloth upon the table was snatched and thrown over the well. Sharp cutting jaws soon had it devoured. Fence posts, hoe and rake handles became whetstones for these voracious pests. Another season of fruitless effort seemed sure.
    Something must be done. What? That hot summer of 1877, in July, the decision was made. Friends, newspapers, and by various means, reports of a new opportunity -- a new place where good management and hard work could retrieve the dwindled finances of these Wetmore, Kansans. But it was far, far away in the Black Hills of Dakota Territory. Tales laden with fool's gold seemed real gold. Gold! -- beyond civilization -- almost. The road was long. Danger lurked on every side. Highwaymen, Indians, and uncertainty. The family, never-the-less, garnered what cash they could from their possessions but kept the farm "just in case". With a sturdy team and two other horses, the Boyces were on the long trek to the distant "Land of Beginning Again" -- the Black Hills of Dakota Territory.
    Their covered wagon was not unlike that of many they met along the way. "Black Hills" was the common topic of conversation. Sometimes they stopped to rest and inquire, often only a nod. The first big rest was taken at Sidney, Nebraska. Here the family wash was done and supplies obtained. At night the campfire was early put out. As the travelers lay on their beds either in the wagon or on the ground, the "Who? Who?" of many owls added to the far-away-from-homeness. Were these calls sign language of Indians? What

did these various silence-breakers mean? Highwaymen? What danger?

    Each morning early, almost before the dawn had pulled the curtain for day, the chug of the rolling wheels over rutted roads began. Distance was eaten up by days. One twilight evening on August 12, 1877, Crook City found the travelers as part of its population. A plan to establish a butcher shop here faded, and John fell a victim of "mountain fever". The prescribed cure was milk. Gold could have been more easily obtained. Sluice gold was quite common then. Twenty miles away near Spearfish was an obtainable cow, according to report. Mother Boyce's sturdy feet carried her in the search. She returned, driving her milk supply ahead of her.

    As soon as John was able to travel, the field looked greener at Central City. Reports had come that it, no doubt, would be the county seat. New claims, new businesses -- more ways to make money. Eleven mills blew their busy blasts morning and evening in Central and Golden Gate, even a foundry added its clamor to these sounds. Other mills in adjoining gulches tooted the joy of their busy-ness. (Vast numbers of grasshoppers flew over even in Dakota.)

    Central City was filled with people. Some were hunting the willow-o'-the wisp-gold; a few came to prey upon the efforts of others; some just on their way. Lawlessness was prevalent and the real Black Hills was eclipsed by these superficial things.

    "There are men in this city who haven't seen the inside of a church for over twenty years. We heard one of them say so, and he wanted to know how the people acted in them gospel shops." (The <u>Black Hills Daily Times</u>: January 25, 1879.)

    It was in Central City that Ellen Charlotte Boyce and Frank S. Bryant were wed and began a home in Pocket Gulch. The vivacious Ellen was all that it takes to make a pioneer. Her friendliness, the keen sense of the funny side, her ability to laugh with others, or to sing away her difficulty made her a "nugget" without price.

    Clear and sweet, her voice mingled with the endless song of the pines as she sang "In the Sweet Bye and Bye" in the moonlight, early dawn, at noon, when she rocked her child to sleep -- no matter how dark the day -- a light came with the prophetic words she sang.

Joy at the birth of her first born, John Sidney, ended after twelve brief days. He went to Mount Moriah in Deadwood to pioneer into another realm. Within another year Matilda Elenora lingered five months before she, too, joined her brother upon the hillside. In 1882, another daughter came. Two years later, a pudgy little brother for Mary stopped at the Bryant household.

In 1884, Carbonate Camp had put its name upon the lips of many. Among those to leave for the Camp were Frank S., Ellen, and their two children, (a babe three-weeks old, also bearing the name Frank).

A snug log house upon the south side of a hill near a spring (the water supply of the town) was the new home. In Carbonate Camp, 1500 male votes were cast, so it was indeed a little city. The main street was lined on either side with houses, many of which were boards nailed to studding. The cracks were covered with battens, a narrow strip of board. The inside was lined with unbleached muslin upon which paper was pasted. At best, these structures were very cold.

Pot-bellied stoves and stoves which held, and consumed, large chunks of wood, kept fire for a time. They must be replenished often. Very fortunate was the one who could "bank" his fire for heat for the entire night.

Sickness in winter was the inevitable in this type of house. Diphtheria, the scourge of children, carried away as many children as five in a single night. Five white bows from five front doors told to the Camp that some child therein had gone. Among all, but especially the older, was pneumonia. A black bow on the door told that death had not come to a child.

Ellen, among other women in the Camp, provided sheets to "lay out" those who were not pioneering here longer. People of the Camp took their turn at "sitting up" with the dead. Friends dug a grave for their friend and walked with him the last trip. Diphtheria victims were taken by a few friends and interred without formality. Perhaps some neighbor read a passage of Scripture; often even this was dispensed with. Getting a coffin from Deadwood was a big task. Treks of twenty miles on foot were sometimes necessary. The mailman brought the casket, and buckboard or sleigh provided the conveyance to the cemetery.

Mrs. Bryant was often called on to "look in" upon an ailing child. She was kind, soft-spoken, dependable, and her judgment was good. One bereft mother came for Ellen to see her seven-year-old son. A glance into the throat and "a doctor at once" was the recommendation. To get the doctor meant a probable walk of ten miles to Central City or two miles further to Deadwood. Folks were good walkers in those days. But even then, the doctor's visit was often too late. In the little cemetery upon the flat beyond the schoolhouse are the bodies of five little ones who could not wait for the doctor.

One cold, winter twilight, a knock came upon the Bryant door. Smithy had come for flowers for seven-year-old Pearl who had gone via "sore throat". The singer of "In the Sweet Bye and Bye" had a green thumb. Nightly, during the long winter, her plants must be taken from the windows and wrapped in paper to avoid freezing. This evening, the plants were down to a few leaves, but lovingly they were snipped and in no time her nimble fingers had made a white velvet calla lily -- the only funeral flower -- but a sheaf of love in the heart that fashioned it.

Gray days came, too. Again in 1890, the baby daughter born five weeks before, died. One pair of kind shoulders, those of John Adams, carried the little white box as the family walked tearfully behind. Mr. Fraev had read "Suffer the Little Children" and a small wreath of pansies fashioned by Edna Goodman went into the opening with the wee girl, remembered as Little Sister. Melody, a lovely, brown-eyed, golden-haired four-year-old went to the "flat beyond the schoolhouse" in 1893. "It is hard to lose a child any time, but harder when they can talk", said the starry-eyed Mother Bryant.

Three weeks after Melody's going, another brown-eyed little girl, Esther, came and softened the loneliness. Later, a serious little boy, Stewart Joseph, came to join the Bryants. "Artist" Leonora came later. The child-bearing period closed with Robert Merrick. Mother Ellen's only regret was that the children were so scattered in their place of abode.

Years of pioneering had taken its toll and, in 1910 Frank S. Bryant went prospecting into another situation. He had been here since August, 1875. Surely he has "struck it" there.

With a zest for the new still in her heart, this native of early Black Hills settlement "took up" a homestead in the Limestone country. Here she and her sons, Stewart and Robert, ranched for several years. Each day was a challenge. The "sweet bye and bye" offered much. When signs that the journey was ending came, she met them with the same song in her heart. After only eighteen months of illness she left us, but surely with the song -- "In the Sweet Bye and Bye".

So, from the banks of the Wabash, to the Black Hills, and again to the Neosho in Kansas, the journey begun by Ellen ended. The willing feet, the understanding heart and the singing voice are away, but as the winds play in the trees, if you listen closely, "In the Sweet Bye and Bye" comes with other sweet tunes from the places where this Ellen Charlotte Boyce Bryant has left her presence.207

Armilda Matherly Gamet Cole
Lawrence County
1878

Her experiences in pioneering began in 1878 when her father, James Matherly, brought his five-year-old daughter, Armilda, to the pioneer town of Deadwood. His wife and baby son had died three years before, and Matherly was devoted to his little daughter and wanted her with him, although it was a rather rugged life for a motherless child.

Matherly had a road-house, or trading post, about ten miles from Deadwood, where he did a good business selling provisions to the Indians. The Indians used mostly bows and arrows in those days, and some of them were not to be trusted.

One day Matherly took his little daughter with him on a trip to Deadwood for a stock of provisions. He had six little black mules to pull the covered wagon and the trail wagon. On the way back with the loaded wagons they came to a long hill that was slick with ice. Matherly decided to take the wagons up the hill one at a time.

"Now Mildy, you stay here with the trail wagon, and I'll be back in a little while and get you," her father told her. The girl waited patiently in the trail wagon. Three wagons loaded with Indian families came along. They could not go up the hill as it was a narrow road with a steep grade on one side and a drop of many feet on the other.

"An old Lakota woman came up and pointed to me, then to her back and up the hill," Armilda recalls. "I was only five or six but I understood her sign language. I climbed on her back and she wrapped her blanket around us, "Lakota child" style, and took me up the hill to Daddy. I thought it was fun but Daddy was provoked and scolded the Indians for taking me".

"Then the Indians offered to trade a most beautiful beaded blanket for me. My Daddy said, 'Why, mercy no! I wouldn't trade her for all the stuff you have.' Daddy scolded me, too, saying that I must never do that again because the Indians steal little white children." The Indians could easily have disappeared into the rough country with the little girl, and she might never have been found.*

"When I was about seven, Daddy told me I could have all the money I made by peddling the surplus milk from the two cows. I remember that I saved up $8.00, which I had in a little buckskin bag. Daddy put the bag away for me with his money. He had his gold and silver coins in a gallon can which he put under the floor in our cabin, and we spread a buffalo rug over the loose floorboards. He cautioned me, "Mildy, you must never tell anyone about this money we have hidden or the Indians or robbers might kill me and take you and the money."

"Our home was the usual, one-room cabin of the time. There were no glass windows, but a couple of boards could be slid open for ventilation. The door was opened by a latchstring, and when I pulled the string inside the cabin nobody could get in. Sometimes Daddy had a woman to look after me, but frequently I was alone, as women didn't care to stay out in the wilderness. I had a little black kitten which I played with when I stayed alone while Father was away."

"Ed Collins, a friend of Father's, convinced him that it wasn't safe to keep me at the trading post because the Indians might steal me or desperadoes might kidnap me for his money. One day father asked, 'How would you like to go back to your Grandma Swalley's?' That suited me fine so he took me to my maternal Pennsylvania Dutch grandmother so I could enter school, as I was now past seven. I entered in the middle of the term and my handsome teacher, George Maule, gave me special help so I could catch up with my class."

"Daddy came back when I was eleven and arranged for me to live with another family as my grandmother had died. Then he left, and I never heard from him or saw him again for sixteen years. By that time I was married and the mother of two children and living on a homestead near Oral. He explained his long absence in this fashion: 'I got married in Kansas City and my new wife was so jealous of you, Mildy, that I couldn't come and get you.'" Matherly still had some of the gold from his Deadwood days. Later his life ended tragically in California when he was murdered -- perhaps for his money. .

"Much had happened to me during my father's absence. I had run away at fourteen and worked out in several homes; then Alma Gamet and I had married on February 11, 1890. We had come by train to Buffalo Gap, and lived on a ranch several miles from the Gap."

"There was great excitement," she recalls, "at the time of the Indians uprising which resulted in the Wounded Knee Massacre about fifty miles from us. The government ordered that the women and children be brought to Buffalo Gap." As she could not be moved to town at that time, thirty neighbors came to help guard the cabin to keep the Indians from setting it on fire. The people were quite concerned about the Indian uprising and rumors of danger were plentiful.

After Mrs. Gamet had been in labor for a day and a half, the woman caring for her sent Grant Brinker to Buffalo Gap for the doctor. The doctor was out, so Brinker waited for him. As they were coming back in the bright moonlight they saw a group of people who called out, "How! How!"

The old doctor cried out to Brinker, "Whip up! Whip up! The Indians are after us." Brinker replied, "I don't believe those are Indians." The doctor snatched up the whip and scared the team, which ran away. The roads were rough and the wheel struck a hole, upsetting the buggy. The doctor and driver were thrown out on the ground but Brinker stopped the horses and the men righted the buggy and eventually arrived at the Gamet Cabin. Meanwhile, the baby had arrived and had been dressed.

When the baby was two weeks old, Gamet hitched his big team to the wagon, and they started to Buffalo Gap. In crossing the Cheyenne River the ice broke, cutting the horses' legs. Finally, with some help from others in the party, they arrived safely at the Gap. Mrs. Gamet and the baby, Johnny, slept on the floor of a cabin which held three other Gamet families.

In a few days the Indians scare quieted down, and they decided they would rather risk being scalped by the Indians than live in such crowded conditions. As their supplies for loading ammunition had come, the Gamets felt that they would be fairly safe at home. It had been necessary for the men to go home and do chores each day.

They lived on the ranch for ten years and were dried-out seven years in a row. Then they went to Sioux City for fourteen years and, after spending one year in Omaha, they returned to Oral. Gamet had become a stock buyer. They had four children. After they parted, Mrs. Gamet married Scott Dulin, but death claimed him in a couple of months. Later on she married James Cole.

Now she is living in Oral where she keeps house of her son, Arthur. Even today she has a black kitten on her doorstep, but it is no relation to the one which kept her company at the Deadwood cabin seventy-three long years ago.208

Annie Rozenkranz Fish
Lawrence County
1878

A Deadwood woman is proud of the fact that six generations of her family have lived in the Black Hills. She is Mrs. Annie Rosencranz Fish and she points out four generations are still living in the Hills.

Annie's grandfather, Sam Kaiser, was born in Switzerland and grew up and married there. The new land of America appealed to the young couple so they crossed the ocean and landed in San Francisco, then moved to Montana.

It was in Montana where they met Henry Rosencranz, who was born in Germany. Kaiser had a young daughter named Lucy, and when she and young Rosencranz met, fate decided their future. They were married in Helena, Montana, and became Annie's parents.

When their two older children were small, the family pulled up Montana stakes and headed for the Black Hills. Rosencranz came into Central City in 1876 when the place was booming.

"I was born in Fort Benton, Montana, and came to the Black Hills in 1877 when I was just a baby. My father had come out in 1876 and had located in Central where he had a saloon.

"My mother and I had been visiting in New York when he sent for us, so we came by train to Sydney, Nebraska, and from there on out to the Black Hills by stagecoach," recalled Mrs. Fish as her crochet hook glinted in and out while she visited.

"My father was always a 'liquor man' from his youth on and he built a large brewery in Central City in 1878. It was not only the first brewery in Central City but also the first one in the Black Hills," said Annie. "It was located down on the creek banks just below the foot-bridge near Golden Gate. The building was frame and there was a separate frame malt house."

"Father used to haul loads of beer to Rapid City, Sturgis, Custer, Keystone, Spearfish and Rochford by wagon and horses. A big wagon, loaded high with wooden kegs filled with beer, sure made the horses tighten their harness tugs. Imagine taking four days to make a trip to Rapid City. That is how long it took my father to make the trip with a load of beer.

He built us a home that was a regular little doll house. It was located in front of the malt-house.

In 1883, the terrible flood washed out the foundation of our home and the house upset in the creek. We managed to get out safely, though, and saved all our furniture. Many stores and houses washed away. I can easily recall seeing that house of ours suddenly weave on its feet, topple upside down, then go sailing like a toy boat down the creek."

"A lot of Central City floated away that time and there were about 10,000 people living in the town at the time. Many of the houses were completely destroyed or lost. Some folks got busy and rebuilt right away, but others never rebuilt at all," recalls Mrs. Fish.

The Rosencranz family found temporary shelter in the Rose Hotel which was located across from where the post office is now. There were two good hotels in the town at the time. When the flood waters subsided, the Rosencranz family moved into the malt house where they lived for a short time.

"You probably think of a malt house as a little bit of a place," said Annie with a smile. But as I recall it, the building was about as large as that building over there." She pointed to the Syndicate building in Deadwood.

Even while they lived in the malt house, business went on as usual. There was a system of heating the hops, and the malt was put into the "warming room" where it would sprout in three days. Then they would beat off the roots and discard them. It was, in reality, quite a complicated process, but Rosencranz was an expert in the beer business, as he brought his knowledge from his fatherland.

When the beer was drawn off, the mash that was left was always dumped into the creek. It smelled to high heaven, of course, and the cows got so they could smell it the minute it was dumped out. They would head straight for the mash pile as fast as they could go. "Did you ever see a drunk cow?" Annie asked with a twinkle in her eyes.

"Well, it was an ordinary sight to see somebody's cow come staggering up from the mash dump. She'd look terribly inflated in the middle and would walk with her legs all spraddled out. Sometimes we'd wonder if the cows would make it home but they always did. Anyway, the owner could have trailed them easily from the milk. As the drunk cow staggered home the milk would be coming in a steady stream from several faucets! Nobody minded the loss of the milk as it was cheap in those days and the drunk cows seemed to be enjoying themselves!"

"The pigs, too, developed a terrible yen for the mash, and would gorge up every chance they got. It wasn't unusual to see a bunch of pigs staggering towards home," Annie recalls.

Beer was big business even in those days and Rosencranz employed seventeen men in his brewery. Most all the beer was put into kegs, and bottles were precious. You never saw broken bottles decorating the road then, as the bottles were saved and reused again and again.

"A big glass of frothy beer cost only a nickel in the saloons and with it went a free lunch. The lunch was really a meal," recalls Annie. It consisted of ham, pickles, potato salad and cheese, and sometimes kraut and wieners went along with it. The lunch and the sociability attracted the trade and the saloons ran day and night."

"I guess maybe people were different in those days," said Annie. "Take the homes, for instance. Nobody locked the door. If you were stranded, you could always find food and shelter. If your absent hosts didn't show up by the time you left, you simply left a note (making sure you had cleaned up the mess), made the bed, and washed the dishes."

"In those years there were many thousands of persons there -- we had fourteen saloons, three butcher shops, three churches. I remember one church was turned into a skating rink. The only prize I ever won in my whole life was there at the rink when I was dressed as a sailor boy."

"There were twenty stamp mills in Central, and prospectors were thick as flies all up and down the creek. Some were just ordinary men, others were rough, tough-bearded guys."

"I guess I would have made a good Indian, I like the outdoors so well, yet as a child I was always sickly."

"It was in Central where I saw my first Indian, and one time my father and my uncle stood guard at both doors of our house to keep the Indians from breaking in. The Indians got discouraged and left."

One near tragedy that stands out in her memory is that of falling into the creek, washing a block downstream before her father caught up with her and rescued her. Rozenkranz, her father, was a big, strong man weighing 220 pounds, and she recalls him lifting her high above the crowd in the first theater in Central, practically stopping the show.

She remembers the old wood chute at the DeSmet mill where great cords of wood came down the chute around the hill to be used in the mills, for in those days everything was of wood, and wood was also used for fuel.

"In 1887 practically everything on Main street in Central burned down when a fire started in a cafe. Central and Terraville hook-and-ladder outfits did their best, but there simply wasn't enough water. For the second time in her childhood, Mrs. Fish saw her home swept away, this time by fire which completely destroyed it and all contents.

"That was when we moved into the malt house at the brewery where my father stored his hops and malt. It was awful -- our home had been so nice with lovely rugs and nice furniture before the fire got it."

"My mother had died, so my two sisters and I were scattered for a time until father could get our house rebuilt. Lots of homes that burned down were never rebuilt," recalls Mrs. Fish.

Central was slowly, but surely disintegrating, so her father retired from the brewery business.

She was married in Central City in 1895 to Albert Fish. "I lived for thirty years in Central. It was there I married Fish, and we had two children. Mr. Fish was a blacksmith and he came in 1878.

He got the gold fever as many men did. He and a group of men went together and leased the land that is now the Terraville ball-field and tried their luck at gold mining. After spending about $10,000 they gave up. Later, Ott Grant, while plowing the land (it was his), discovered a very rich vein of gold. It was so much that he was a millionaire in a short time.

After she was married, she had many more exciting experiences. She rode on the Burlington Train when it made its first trip to Lead. It was here Calamity Jane asked a boy to kiss her and he wouldn't. Calamity then told him that later on he'd wished he had. It didn't make much difference to the boy as he died a short time later.

They moved to Spearfish and lived there for a number of years. Her husband died in 1933. Mrs. Fish spent several years in Colorado, Texas and California. She was housekeeper at the Brown Palace Hotel in Denver for four years and later went to Texas where she operated the first tourist court in the state. She returned to the Hills from California to be with her daughter in Terraville. She made her home in Deadwood for the past twelve years. She had been housekeeper at the Pineview for three years.

"I've lived in Deadwood for twenty years and travelled in a dozen different states," said Mrs. Fish with a laugh. "But I must like the Hills for I always came back."

"I like to cook, but just think of food prices! Why, in those early years we got hams for ten cents a pound, coffee for ten cents and sugar for $4.00 a hundred pounds. Wages in the mines were $2.50 a day, sometimes $3.00. We were just as well off then as now -- we did manage to save a little money then," said Mrs. Fish. 209

Laura Belle Gamut
Fall River County
[before 1889]

New Land in Dakota

After our boy, Worth, was born, the menfolk began to talk more and more of the new land being opened up in Dakota; how rich it was, how one could obtain it by just going through certain procedures with Uncle Sam. That fall, my father and brothers and Joe and his father and brothers went out to Dakota to take a look.

It was all as good and as promising as they had been led to believe. And in February -- February has always been an eventful month for me -- my sister with her two small children, my baby boy, and I joined the menfolk.

It was a beautiful day, that day the men unloaded the stock car, the car with the household goods, and the car with provisions and stock. They unloaded at Buffalo Gap, twelve miles northwest of the land our men had selected. This was then Dakota Territory. That fall the twin states were admitted. Both of us were young, South Dakota and Laura Belle Gamet. I had so much to learn, as a pioneer, homesteading wife.

We had moved into an earlier settler's shanty, to stay while the men were building a small house for us. Everything had to be hauled out and the drivers had to ford the Cheyenne River.

"Well, well, that's something I sure didn't want to see," Joe exclaimed, peering out the door a few days after we had moved into the settler's shanty. "What is it, coyotes?" I asked, coming close to him, and peeping over his shoulder. "No, snow. We just don't need any snow right now." Sure enough, the air was white with big, soft flakes and it fell until there was a foot of snow on the ground. Not a very heavy fall, but very unwelcome, for all our fuel and water had to be hauled from a distance.

Surveyors

No sooner had the snow disappeared than Joe's father came in with the news that the surveyors would probably be in some time that day. We could not build until they had surveyed the land and we could be sure we were getting our houses and barns on our own acres.

"Think you can cook for these men, Honey?" Joe asked. "I mean with your sister's help, of course." "Why, I'm sure I can. How many will there be in their outfit?" "Oh, five or six, I imagine," Joe replied, lightheartedly. "But we have no table at which they can be seated," I told him, for only a part of our household goods had come out, enough with which to start housekeeping.

"Shucks, they won't care whether they're sitting down at a table or sitting out there under the sky, with a big plate of food in their hands, just so you cook plenty of good, hearty food. Grub, they call it."

"What about sleeping arrangements, Joe?" "Thank goodness your mother made you a great pile of quilts and you've pieced some yourself. We have plenty of covering. We'll just fix up beds right on the floor," Joe told me.

So we did, and the surveyors seemed to like my big helping of pickled ham or pork shoulder and potatoes. With Joe's help, I baked light bread every day. I must have been a pretty good breadmaker even then, for there was never a crumb left on the plates.

Fortunately it did not become very cold while that first crew of men were staying with us. By early March our little one-room house on Joe's claim was finished and we moved in, as happy as kings.

Worth, our two-year-old, explored every cranny and corner, as two-year-olds will, laughing up at me as if he thoroughly approved.

A few months later, our second boy, Ward, was born. Joe had broken some sod and planted corn, so we felt that life had really begun in this new country.

Looking for Rain

Each morning we would stand in front of our little prairie home, looking up into the skies for some sign of rain. Joe shook his head, as if to shake off the sight of eternal blue skies. "It is just simply what is known as a dry year," he remarked, as the season advanced.

One day Father Gamet came in, with a determined look on his face. "I'm going back to Iowa where I KNOW the corn is growing as high as your head, and I'll see that you children have some corn. I'll ship out a carload," he said. And he did.

We did not raise anything, not even a garden to speak of, that summer. While we were waiting for the carload of corn to arrive, we would gather in front of one of our little one-room cabins and sing and tell stories, mostly for the children's benefit. Sometimes we would tell them about people of another generation, who, like us, had experienced hardships of a settler, but had outridden the storm.

Making New Friends
There was great rejoicing when our carload of shelled corn arrived. Now we were able to get through the rest of the summer. But with fall days, illness came, too. My father was stricken. It was decided to take him to his old home in Iowa. My sister and her family went with him, to care for him. My brother, who had taught the first school in our community, decided to return, too. In fact, almost all the people who had come when we did, decided that fall to return to Iowa. How we missed those kinsfolk and friends that first winter!

"Here's a letter from one of our old neighbors in Iowa. He wants to know if we would like to trade him our Iowa home. Says he'll trade us seventy-five head of cattle for the place. What shall we tell him?" Joe asked. We looked at each other silently. It was hard to make up our minds to part with that little house, which had been our very first home. But, after all, this was our home now, out here in the Dakotas, and what we could do with seventy-five head of cattle!

"Let's make the trade, Joe," I said. Joe kissed me, and gave me a big hug. "You'll never be sorry," he said. "Just be patient. I know you miss your folks and all your schoolgirl friends, but some day before long, as this new country becomes settled, you'll find you have more friends than you ever had before."

He was right. I have looked forward many times to visiting our folks in Iowa, but neither of us ever cared to go back there to live. We have had ups and downs, sometimes I think more downs than ups, but somehow we managed to come out on top. I have raised our four boys on the prairies, all four good men, and I am thankful we made up our minds to stay.

Visits by Indians

It was a long time before we had visits from anyone except our Indian neighbors. Living on the trail leading from Pine Ridge Reservation to what is now our county seat, Hot Springs, we were constantly seeing groups of these first settlers on their way to the place where they had bathed in the springs for untold years. Many times I was alone with my small children, Joe and the other men being at fields far from home, when I would look out and notice tents pitched in front of the house.

I would never hear them come, especially when our window and door were closed. They came so quietly and put up their tents so quickly and as quietly. Later in the day, some of these wayfarers would open the door and walk in, their moccasins giving no warning of their visit. Perhaps I was kneading bread or washing diapers. I would turn and there would be several red-skinned visitors. I would offer them chairs. They would sit beside the fire and just sit there, saying nothing. No word at all, unless it was to request something by Indian words, signs, and gestures.

Once three or four men stopped on their way to Hot Springs. As was often the case, only I and the babies were at the house when they walked in. After sitting silently for fifteen or twenty minutes, the older man asked for "wakalyapi." He pointed to a shelf where I kept groceries and a few pots and pans. But I did not know what "wakalyapi" was. I picked up several objects, holding them out to him. He shook his head each time. Finally he pointed to the coffee pot.

I thought he must want coffee, so I put a pound of coffee in a paper sack. Wrapping it carefully, tying it with a bit of strong twine, I handed it to him. My visitor shook his head even more vehemently than before. He showed me by gestures, imitating the way water is poured into a coffee pot, and blowing on the coals to make fire burn, that he wanted me to make some coffee. So I made a pot of coffee and poured out a cup for each of the guests.

"Canhanpi," grunted the older one this time. He looked around, saw the sugar dish and pointed to it. I gave them sugar for their coffee, serving them from the blue-and-white sugar dish which had been one of our wedding presents.

"Asanpi," the old Indian demanded now, smiling broadly and pointing to a covered pail of milk near the stove. I was glad it was not yet sour, as I hastily poured some into a small glass pitcher and took it to them.

But that was not all. The next request was for "aguyapi," which I did not know at that time meant bread. It was easy to understand, though, when he showed the form of a bread loaf and motioned as if slicing it. This time I opened the oven and broke off great pieces of bread which I had baked for a previous meal.

After they had finished their bread and coffee, one of the men walked to the shelf and poured the remaining coffee into his pouch, so as to take it with him. He reached into his wallet, took out a handful of silver, and paid me. Then they walked out, got on their horses and rode away to Hot Springs.

"And weren't you frightened?" one of my little nieces once asked. Indeed, no. I have been accustomed to Indians all my life, and have never had reason to fear them. They were always our friends. Even as a child in Iowa, the Winnebagos would come to work in the timber. I was taught always to be kind to them, as they often came to the house to trade. I have tried always, too, to remember they were on this land long before any of us came. They never made much trouble until soldiers tried forcing them away from their beloved hills, their abundance of wild game, and sheltering woods.

Indian Outbreak

I recall the year of the Indian outbreaks [1890], when the government issued guns and ammunition to our settlers, ordering all women and children taken to Buffalo Gap, where soldiers were stationed. Two of the neighbors had new babies, but they put beds in the wagons, placed mothers and babies in the beds, and drove to Buffalo Gap -- twelve rutty miles, and the Cheyenne river to ford.

Little damage resulted from this outbreak. At the end of the trouble, it was found the Indians had killed some of our cattle for food. We have been friends with the Indians since then.

What I admired about the Indians was their custom in regard to killing game. They never killed for sport, as some white men do. They dried their meat and kept it for winter use, using the skins for robes, tents, and shoes. Sometimes I think of those soft robes when I see the deer today, jumping our fences, and seeming to come and go at will in our ranch pastures.

Other Strange Guests

Other unexpected visitors came to the claim shack besides Indians. We had not suspected running into a snowstorm one winter night when we came home from a distant neighbor's, and we were not uneasy, even though we realized we would be getting home much later than planned.

"These faithful horses know every step of the way; we can trust them. Just settle down into the lap robe and doze, if you like," Joe told me. The way home seemed longer that night, but finally I said, "Joe, we are almost to the edge of Hay Canyon. I believe I recognize some of the landmarks." He looked at his watch. It was after midnight, but now I was sure I could see the dim outlines of our home, the barns, and sheds. Sure enough, in a few minutes Joe was driving into the yard.

He went to the barn, put up the tired horses, and I opened the door. We never locked the door. I laid the baby, still fast asleep, in his crib, so my hand would be free to light the lamp. My hands were so cold, I could hardly turn up the wick. As I looked down at our bed, I saw, to my astonishment, that it was already occupied, and occupied by a total stranger.

The man sat up now, rubbing his eyes and looking very sheepish and embarrassed. To Joe and me (for Joe came in just about this time) he explained that he had lost his way in the storm and sought shelter at our place. "There was no one at home," he explained. "I took off my wet boots, made up the fire, and dried myself. Still no one came in, so I fried some eggs and made a hoecake. By the time I had washed the dishes, I decided there was probably no one coming in tonight, so I turned in."

We all had a hearty laugh at this point. Passing cattlemen often stopped with us, but this was the first time we had come in to discover one calmly sleeping in our bed. We made up a pallet on the floor. Our visitor spent the rest of the night with us, ate a hearty breakfast next morning, and rode off at sunrise, headed for Buffalo Gap.

Wolves

Only two of us are left of the original settlers who came to this bit of what was then Dakota Territory, Mrs. Will Tice and I. We have enjoyed life together, have been good friends and neighbors, and today share most of our letters and share news on the party telephone line.

"Do you remember," the conversation will often begin. "Do you remember the gray wolves coming down from the mountains and killing so many of the cattle and some horses?" In those early days, we were often desperate. Every few days we would find another horse, foal, or calf carried off by treacherous wolves.

"The boys are organizing a hunt," my boy once said excitedly. "Bet we get a gray wolf before we go to bed tonight." They went many times on these expeditions. One day I met the boys at the door. They had been a long way in the mountains that time. "Did you kill a gray wolf today?" I asked. "We killed seven!" they answered. Finally all wolves were driven out. Since then, we have not been bothered with them.

Outriding Storms

"This is a beautiful picture," a ranch visitor remarked, looking across grainfields stretching before us like a golden carpet. "It is beautiful," I agreed. "And I hope it will look just like it is now until we get it harvested and safely in the barns," for I was thinking of the hailstorm that came like a thief one summer night, just as our crops were ready to harvest. The hail beat the grain into the ground and wind blew the straw out of the field. Then rain followed the hail, and soaked the ground. However, the grain sprouted, thus making food for livestock, and our rye started a crop for next year.

In 1911, we decided to build a large barn for our hay and a place for twelve horses. "What a summer this is," my boys often said. "Dry! dry! dry!"

"We'll have a good soaking rain some day soon," I would answer stoutly. But I was wrong. We never had that rain, and we did not raise even as much as one load of hay to put in the new barn. The corn, planted in May, did not come up until August. We sold all our cattle at low prices that fall, but we could hardly sell the horses at any price. When World War I began, prices for horses were better. We started raising horses. We sold many for cavalry horses. A few years later, we went to California. I left my dear Joe out there. We buried him in California. I came back to the ranch to find it badly run down and in need of repairs. But the boys and I started in with a right good will.

In spite of wolves, drought, and hail, we have outridden the storm. "Prairie Belle," Uncle Joe called me, because when he was a Mississippi River boat captain, he had known a Prairie Belle steamboat. "You're just like that boat," he often told me. "Nothing could stop her, not even an earthquake that threw water into high waves. She weathered those high waves and nothing could stop her."210

A dance hall girl from the Black Hills.
Photo taken in the 1880's.

Mattie Curtis Jennings
Lawrence County
1876

Part First

The old Concord coaches had three seats. On the one in front, the passengers rode backwards but it was considered the most comfortable, then across from door-to-door was a seat and a wide leather strap across for the back, and the back seat. Each seat held three grown people. We had nine inside and two with the driver. Our baggage was in the boot under the driver's seat. We had four horses which were changed every twenty miles. When getting near a place to change, the driver gave a piercing yell, and when we drove in, the horses were ready to be put right on, and away we went.

The first night we drove all night. We always stopped for our three meals each day, ready for us where we changed horses and we always made it on time when the roads were good, but if it rained and we got into gumbo, it was a different story. The second night we got to Fort Robinson (where Crawford is now), and two brothers named Deer were opening a hotel for coach passengers. Our driver decided we would stay there all night. The driver of a coach was in full command, so the house was completed but rooms not in order, but they put up beds and made us comfortable.

Mrs. Dawson came to my room while hers was put in order. There were no curtains at the window and Mrs. Dawson had taken off her blouse to freshen up and saw Indians looking in at the window, (it was an Indian Reservation at that time) and she said, "Oh, look at those Indian women looking at us," and I said, "They don't happen to be women," which threw her into a panic. I had lived in Iowa where we often had Indians, but she knew nothing of them.

We made an early start and drove most of the next night, but our driver decided to stop from about three in the morning and wait for daylight, as it was raining and the roads were getting a little heavy, so we had two hours rest. The stock-tender gave Mrs. Dawson and me his bed, and General Dawson and Dr. Jennings had a buffalo robe on the floor by our bed. We were getting settled when we found a man feeling around under our pillows. It turned out that he was looking for a clean towel, which one of the passengers had demanded.

The next day, the roads were a little wet and we got into Buffalo Gap about midnight, and there we left the coach to go to Custer where Doctor had to collect revenue. So the coach went on to Deadwood without us. The stock-tender had a two-room cabin; one room was a saloon and the other was his kitchen and bedroom, no door, but a blanket hung between the rooms. Dr. Jennings and our host were out looking after our baggage, and I was alone in the kitchen when the blanket was pulled aside, and a terrible-looking man looked in. I flew out where my husband was, and I had no more than got there, when two men jumped out of the saloon door very close to me in a fight, and our host said to me, "You better go in, they may shoot!" So I flew in faster than I had flown out. The bad-looking man turned out to be "Laughing Sam", called that because his cheek had been cut down to the corner of his mouth, showing his teeth and making him look as if he were laughing.

We had to get to Custer, so a team and two-seated spring wagon was brought around by an old driver and our baggage was put in, and the driver said, "Put the lady in," and I was put in, and away we went. I said, "Aren't you going to take the men?" (There was another man to go) and he said, "Oh, yes, we will come back for them. If I should keep the horses waiting, they might not start again today." I said, "Why, aren't they gentle?" and he said, "Well, they are broncs, and the one of them hasn't been driven this winter, and I don't know as the other one has ever been driven." We got to Point of Rocks for noon dinner. The place is now called Pringle, named that when the Burlington railroad was built through there. We stopped at a cabin where a man was living alone. He prepared our meal, which consisted of venison and hot biscuits. I saw him make the biscuits, so I ate venison. Our broncs made good time and about four o'clock we arrived in Custer City, the broncs on the gallop up the wide street and large flakes of snow falling, May 1, 1877. There we found a nice hotel and it looked good to me, but finding that Laughing Sam was in town did not add to my comfort.

Dr. Jennings was at the time Collector of Government Internal Revenue, and there was no bank in Custer, so he had to take the money to Deadwood to deposit it. We stayed there a week, so did Laughing Sam, and we left for Deadwood on the Cheyenne Coach. One other passenger wanted to send a guard with us but Doctor said, "No," and told the driver if we were held up, to stop, and not risk his life and ours by trying to get away. Well, it was a rainy night, and when we got to Mountain Meadow Ranch, the driver said he couldn't take the coach on to Deadwood and we stayed at the ranch that night and went on next morning in a dead-ex wagon, getting to Deadwood at noon. Our shadow, Laughing Sam, was there ahead of us, so we escaped him by stopping overnight at Mountain Meadow and I have wondered since if the driver of the coach didn't do it for his own, and our, safety.

When our wagon was driven up to the hotel in Deadwood, we were greeted by Judge Bennett who brought his family soon from Yankton, and we became life-long friends.

Part Second

So, I came into Deadwood early in May, 1877. We had to stay at the hotel, which I think was called the Grand Central, kept by a German couple named Wagner. Mrs. Wagner was a character, and took it upon herself to look after me, realizing, I am sure, that in my youth and inexperience I needed care.

The great event of the day was the arrival of the Sidney coach. At their last stop before getting to Deadwood, they put six white horses on and came up the street to the hotel with horses trotting and the driver cracking his whip and blowing a horn.

The bedrooms being very small, I sat in the parlor, and Mrs. Wagner would come to the door to see who had come in, and she seemed to know at once if the arrivals were not what they should be and if they were attempting to talk with me, she would shake her head, and I knew I was not to encourage any familiarity. There were things happening all day and all night that were interesting, if quite disturbing to a country girl. The streets were so crowded with men that a lady hesitated about going out alone.

When I look back at that time, in 1877, I wonder at the great number of fine people who came to the new mining town, families who made their homes there, raised their families and stayed all of their lives. There are few of them left, but many grandchildren, so the names are still with us.

In the winter of '78 there was an epidemic of mountain fever and no hospital to care for the sick men, so a group of women got to work and started a small hospital, rented a small room, put in three beds and hired a man to take care of the sick. We had many donations, and I had my first contact with our blessed Bishop Hare.[*] I don't remember that I was the treasurer of the organization but Bishop Hare got my name and sent a check for ten dollars to be used in the hospital.

After two weeks in the hotel, we moved into our home and I began my feeble effort at housekeeping. We had our furniture sent out from the States, knocked down and had it put up and finished in Deadwood, and it was not easy to get housekeeping utensils. I used a beer bottle for a rolling pin, and I still think with gratitude of the help I had from women who knew how to cook and many other things.

We had a lot of good times, for there was a kindred feeling among the "Old Timers". I say that no one who came into the Black Hills on the railroad can look back upon those days as hardships, for we were young, and there were few dull days in Deadwood during the time I lived there. There were many saloons and gambling houses, and many men and women of the underworld, but it never seemed to interfere in any way with other people. The line between, in no place, was more sharply drawn.

During the summer of '77 my husband and I went down to Crook City (one of the first towns in the Hills but long ago become a ghost town) for the weekend, and Sunday afternoon the men decided to drive down to where an old Bismarck friend of theirs had taken up a ranch with a nice spring on it. So we went in a two-seated spring wagon. We found the place, but their friend was not there. His name was George Bosworth, and the ranch is where the town of Sturgis now is, and I am told that the name of Bosworth is heard there, Bosworth Street, I think. We went on to where Fort Meade now is to get a view of Bear Butte. When we got back to Crook City, we found that some Indians had been near and run off some stock and before the next Sunday, a family named Murray was killed by Indians near where we had been at Bear Butte.

Part Third
In late summer of 1881, Dr. Jennings saw an article in the <u>Deadwood Pioneer</u> (owned and published by Al Merrick, a friend of ours) saying that Mr. Thornby had been through the Black Hills with Professor Jenny and had come across a place in the Southern Hills in Custer County, a spring and creek of warm water. Mr. Merrick said he knew nothing about it more than was in the paper, and said Doctor better see Thornby, which he did, and Thornby said it was true, and the Indians were coming there for baths as it was said to be medicinal.

Dr. Jennings decided to investigate the place, and I was sent to my home in Iowa, and he went to the southern Hills. He was so impressed that he brought Dr. A.S. Stewart to see it, and the result was that they formed a company of five. The land had been filed upon by a white man with an Indian wife. The company bought the man out, and Dr. Jennings proved up on the land and turned it over to the Hot Springs Company. Considered naming the town Minnekahta, which means "hot water" in the Sioux language, but finally decided to call it Hot Springs, and so it stands.

Dr. came to Iowa in the spring of '82 and brought me and our little girl to Hot Springs, and it has been my home ever since. There was a log cabin at the spring where the baths were given, the first hotel and hospital, although we did not dignify it by those names. Four large rooms in a line, one with four beds where the men were put when taking the baths. My room (we had no place for women but I took a few into my room), a dining room and kitchen.

I had a cook, when one could be found; if not, I did the cooking. We generally had from two to six men taking the baths. The spring was where the warm water came out of a hill right into a rock formation that made a good bathtub, large enough for a good-sized person to lie in and let the warm water run over him.

Our bath house was a log cabin about ten by ten with a little wood stove in it and finally, as we became known, people began coming, and gradually we became a town.

The first good hotel built by the Hot Springs Company was the Minnekahta, a very attractive frame building. It burned in 1892 and the Evans Hotel was built on the ground where the

Minnekahta stood, and it still stands. The two hotels were built on the ground where we had our garden.

The Northwestern Railroad came into Hot Springs in 1891 and the Burlington came later. We were a thriving little town; many hotels and homes and business houses were built. Our hotels were full of people taking the baths, and we were in fair way to become a second Arkansas Hot Springs.

The Plunge Bath was built and put into operation in 1891 and is still a popular place, but some doctors came in who did not help advertise the water, and our town was hurt. There have been many attempts to bring back the interest and faith in the water, and I still hope it may be done.

When we came to Hot Springs, all the country south and east was open range, and large companies ran cattle there, so we saw a lot of the cowboys. As our town grew and families came in with young lady daughters, the town was very popular with the boys, and when the settlers began coming and fencing the land, the cattle had to be taken out, but several of the cowboys married and made their homes and raised large families, and their grandchildren are still here with families of their own, and the names are among our best citizens.

The early cowboys were mostly from Texas, but many young men from eastern cities were among them, boys who wanted to go west, and a nice lot of boys they were, and we liked to have them for friends. In those days, there was always some danger that the Indians might make trouble, and we were sure that the boys would come to us if we needed them, and our nearest troops were miles away, and the Indians feared the cowboys as they didn't have to wait for orders from Washington to protect themselves.211

LAWRENCE COUNTY

Clarabelle Liggett Pouriea
1893

"My husband, who had been here since 1879, was the first man to freight fruit trees into the Hills. He hauled them from Sydney, Nebraska, by way of a team and wagon over roads that seemingly had little excuse to even be called roads."

The Pourieas ran a cream station in Central City and also handled some groceries. They were in the ice business for a number of years.

"We had three ponds from which we cut the ice. People had to have ice in those days as Frigidaires* were unknown. They often used to comment to us, 'After all, God makes your ice crop and all you have to do is cut it," explained Mrs. Pouriea with a laugh.

"Our three ice wagons, motored by sweating horses, delivered ice to Terraville, Central City and Lead. The stamp mills were running then and everything always looked so dirty."

"Our place was called the Deadwood Dairy. My husband bought seventy gallons of milk every day and put it out in quarts for sale. In my younger years I had long auburn hair and it used to be a popular joke when folks would say, 'Let's scalp her.'"

"We had dances in the homes -- old time dances, only they were not called that then. Any house that could muster an organ or violin was good for a dance any time."

"My husband placer-mined for twelve years in Blacktail Gulch and had four men working for him. He sold his gold to the bank and it used to be my job to hire a hack and take the gold down to Deadwood.212

Mariah Jane Williams Ford
1878

I never knew whether it was the lure of gold or the urge for new horizons and frontiers that prompted my father to come to the Black Hills. At any rate, my father entered into a partnership with a man who was supposed to have a producing mine in Spruce Gulch. My father's part was to furnish a stamp mill, which was brought into Deadwood by bull teams. Of course it cost a pretty penny. The mine was one of those dreams that did not come true. The bubble burst and left us bankrupt.

Before my mother, brother and I came, which was in 1878, my father built a small house on Charles Street. Here we made our home for many years. We left a sheltered home with everything that our hearts could wish, to come to this very modest home, where we learned to pioneer.

Although the house was small, my mother made it homey with the things she had. All our drinking water was carried from a spring in the gulch above. Barrels of rainwater and melted snow provided water for washing clothes. In later years a well was dug on the back of the lot. Although my mother was very homesick for her old home, she showed wonderful fortitude in meeting the situation, and in time, inspired the whole family to help to better their conditions.

My brother was a great help. From the time he was twelve years old he earned all of his living and helped increase the family income. He delivered the <u>Pioneer Times</u> to the whole town. He was always my champion and protector. Once he earned four dollars and fifty cents by sawing wood, to buy me a lovely doll buggy. He sold bouquets of wildflowers, which my mother arranged, to the saloons for fifty cents. He saved sixteen dollars from selling flowers and bought two shares of Homestake stock at eight dollars per share.

At one time we owned a cow, thus furnishing the family with milk. We also had some regular milk customers. There was a vacant lot next to us where we raised a garden. In season we picked wild raspberries and sold part of them. My mother made jelly and canned many quarts of fruit. We also picked strawberries at Peck's garden.

My mother was most resourceful, made the most of everything she had. She was an excellent and economic cook. I don't think anyone could make better bread. She made, and sold, bread and rolls to add to the household income. Fortunately, mother was clever at sewing, also. She made nearly all of our clothes. She made things out of old things; her rag-bag was a magician's bag. Sometimes she would exchange work for material. She did this very often with our friend Mrs. Smith who lived up Charles Street. Clara Smith and I used to like to play lady, so Mrs. Smith offered to buy material to make some lady dresses if my mother would make them. Mother made us the prettiest long dresses with trains and did we ever have fun with them.

So many people wanted mother to sew for them, which she did for many years for one-dollar-and-fifty-cents a day. When she had enough she invested in something that would earn something. Mother also knit socks, stockings, mittens and leggings. I can never remember my mother sitting idle, she always had something to do.

She was determined that Ed and I should have an education, for she always said it was something no one could take from us. So, when my father wanted to go on a farm, she was determined not to take us out of school. We both finished Deadwood High School. With her industry and thrift she saved enough money to send me to Northwestern University for two years. By work and investment she saved enough to build a house, which she rented for thirty-five dollars per month.

She was always ready to aid people when they were in trouble. At one time there was a scarlet fever epidemic and many children died. Most people were afraid of the disease. She went to many families and helped nurse the children back to health.[213]

Christina Anderson Frawley
1877

Christina was seven years old when her Danish parents decided to leave Yankton to establish their new home in the Black Hills. Many arguments ensued among this couples' Scandinavian friends, but this did not deter the hearty young couple from planning to go the Black Hills, inasmuch as the last treaty had been signed with the Indians. These same friends later helped Katrina and James, in the early spring of 1877, to pack as much as possible into four wagons for the westward trek, and also assisted to start off the many extra men, who were to drive the cattle and horse herds.

Men flocked to the Andersons' to ascertain whether they could help on their trip. A man was willing to hire for his transportation and keep -- demanding no wages -- the great desire was to reach the Black Hills, where they would find gold. Thus, what mattered the time and hardships on such a trip!

In these wagons, carefully packed, was an Estey upright piano. James Anderson was an accomplished musician and he hoped his little daughter, Christina, would have this talent. There, too, were many fine pieces of Victorian furniture: marble-top dressers and tables, besides high-top wooden beds, all skillfully made.

Enroute from Yankton to the Black Hills, on one moonlight night, one of the men accompanying the James Anderson party thought he saw Indians among the horses. He immediately notified Mr. Anderson; at once all the men surrounded the horses -- it proved to a false alarm, as the flies were bothering the horses and in the moonlight, the movement of their heads with the manes bobbing up and down, side-ways too, looked like Indian war bonnets.

Another tale: Christina's mother brought her favorite rocking chair. In the evening around the campfire, Katrina would have her rocker, and often rocked her small daughter. This group dared not sing in fear of attracting the Indians or highwaymen -- so for relaxation and enjoyment, James Anderson would play his violin around the fire after a hazardous days' journey.

James Anderson was responsible for bringing to this new country, ten miles northeast of Deadwood, many of his wife's relatives; giving them a start on his own ranch, and further helping them establish a ranch of their own. Mr. Anderson was always willing to offer prudent advice, and many times was sought for, to act as an counselor.

There had arisen a great need for a school in this Dry Creek area. The stone schoolhouse was built about 1887, and children walked over four miles to this school until later schools were built nearer to their homes.

Christina's early childhood life on this pioneer ranch was sort of a solitary one. True, she assumed certain household duties; she became an avid and experienced horsewoman. Often after completing small chores for her father, she would begin to study and enjoy the phenomena and beauty of nature. The birds were her playmates, she knew them all by name; and the many wild flowers that graced their property typified a personal art gallery for her. Often, on a clear night she would study the grandeur and mystery of the sky -- became quite proficient -- and as she grew older, was very well-versed in the science of astronomy.

She, too, recalled how the scattered bands of Indians that roamed the Hills surrounding their home would uniquely communicate with each other. How eerie it was to observe how the Indians would signal from the hill-tops -- fire signals at night and smoke signals during the day. It was always on such occasions that the men milking their cows had a rifle nearby. Her father, during the early days, hired an Indian scout, thereby someone was able to converse freely with the Indians, and often a few bold warriors would approach the ranch home. On each occasion they were merely hungry and wanted some food. A good meal would be prepared, and these Indians would subsequently be rounded up and escorted to Ft. Meade by the soldiers; there, cared for under military regulations and later transferred to the reservation.

The closest call the family ever experienced for a casualty, was on the occasion that her father sold $1200.00 worth of cattle to a local buyer in Deadwood. Mr. Anderson, before departing for home, often noticed four strange men that kept sort of a mysterious watch on his whereabouts while he remained in town. On his way home, the more he thought about it, the more suspicious he became; he readily decided rather than go directly home, to detour to Whitewood on the Crook City road, and safely there, he deposited the money in the local bank.

The next morning while making his customary trip to Deadwood, he was stopped about one-half mile from his home by these same men. They rapidly searched him personally, and also the contents of the wagon. Finding very little money, they roughly tied him to a tree, whereupon angrily and hurriedly they departed for the ranch home. It so happened that the hired men, six in number, were eating breakfast. These men were ordered outside and lined up near the house. Searching them and the premises, they were only able to find a few dollars and a gold watch. In disgust, as they left, they went to the barn, took three horses and departed towards Whitewood. Among the good horses stolen was Christina's favorite horse, and it proved a very personal loss for her. At the time she was attending school in Spearfish. As these highwaymen left, the leader called

out, "you better, in a half an hour, go down the road and untie your boss."
As soon as they dared, three of the Anderson men went to the location, found Mr. Anderson securely tied to a tree and slightly bruised. Evidence of an overnight campfire and the general markings at the site, proved that these robbers had spent many, many hours at this location waiting for the coming of Mr. Anderson. That day Mr. Anderson did not make his trip to Deadwood -- he delegated his foreman, one Charley Thompson, for the trip, and he was instructed to notify the sheriff. As soon as possible, Christina's father with three of his men endeavored to locate the robbers' trail and, better still, their whereabouts. They looked carefully in the region between St. Onge and Whitewood; but to no avail. In fact, the local police authorities were not able to locate them. Mr. Anderson and his men were extremely anxious to recover Christina's horse -- her father especially, knew and realized how dear the horse was to his daughter. In fact, none of the horses were found; they all knew that the horses would be traded at the nearby towns, as such characters desired money rather than the chattel.214

Alvina Schleichardt Parsons
1889

In 1890 an epidemic of diphtheria swept Lead which caused the death of my brother, leaving me the only child.
My father sold our home and bought a pair of horses, a covered wagon, a tent, and camping equipment and we started out to tour the southern Black Hills in hopes of finding gold and locating a claim. At that time I was nearly seven years old and had two younger sisters.
Our itinerary took us into Wyoming, where in our attempt to ford the Cheyenne river near Newcastle we were caught in a 'flash flood' and everything in our wagon was soaked, including us. A rancher invited us to stay at his home, which we did, until the flood subsided and our bedding dried out.
My father, discouraged at not finding gold, decided to go into the cattle business. We then went to the northern plains of South Dakota and bought a ranch, including three-hundred head of cattle, on the north fork of the Moreau river in Harding county.

To get there, we traveled one hundred miles north of Belle Fourche on a gumbo road. If the weather was dry it took us about three days. If we were caught in a rain we stayed where we were until the roads dried, as it was impossible to travel in the gumbo.

During our first year there we had a late winter blizzard and many a newborn calf was brought in, wrapped in blankets, and revived by pouring whiskey down its throat.

When spring opened it was necessary to buy food and ranch supplies at Dickinson, North Dakota. Upon returning, the wagon which my father was driving was hit by a large cake of ice. The wagon overturned and nearly all the supplies were washed away. Some of the supplies were recovered miles down the river.

In the fall we came to Spearfish as there were no schools near the ranch. There I entered the first grade in the red brick school house, at the age of eight. My father sold the cattle ranch and bought a horse ranch in the Cave Hill country near Ludlow. Many of these horses were sold as cavalry horses for the Spanish American War.215

The main street of Deadwood at the beginning of white settlement in 1876.

MEADE COUNTY

Jessie Gannon Handlin Keene
1887

During the "Prairie Days" of 1898 to 1908, Jessie was a school teacher in Meade County. In 1898, she taught the Grashul school in District 31. She and her twelve-year-old brother, Ed, rode horseback fifteen miles from their home on the Belle Fourche River. This term ran from September 12 to December 2. Then the term started again from April 10 to June 30, with sixteen pupils. The wages were $35.00 per month.

One of the happy incidents Effie recalled is a trip to Sturgis with Jessie, in a one horse buggy. The horse Jessie drove was balky, so sometimes gave her a bad time.

Effie told me she never saw a more beautiful sight than the one they saw as they drove up Alkali Creek over the hill into Fort Meade. The soldiers were all out on the prairie, drilling. The sunset in the distance was gorgeous. Just a beautiful mass of glowing color. They were jaunting up the road in front of "Soap Suds Row" singing, "Sweet Bunch of Daisies," and just as Jessie hit the highest note in the song, the buggy hit a rock, and threw her out. A bit shaken, but not badly injured, she scrambled up to get the horse stopped. He definitely wasn't balky then, and I bet furnished some entertainment for the folks living by the roadside.

The non-commissioned officers, many of whose wives did the laundry for some of the garrison soldiers, lived by this road, northwest of Fort Meade, just south of Bear Butte Creek. It would be north of today's highway location. Every day of the week there were clothes hanging on the lines, all washed by hand on the board or in a wooden washing machine operated by hand. This lane of houses was known as "Soap Suds Row."

In 1901 Jessie married Charles S. Handlin of Hereford. Charles filed a homestead where the Cross S Outfit ran part of their cattle. After ranching for a couple of years, Charles became ill with what they later thought was tuberculosis. Jessie went back to teaching another rural school, this time in District 79 with nineteen pupils. The wages were still $35.00 per month. Some of the boys were eighteen years old, and older. In 1904

and 1905 Jessie taught in District 85. The wages were still $35.00 but she had only seven pupils.
Charles Handlin became seriously ill, so Jessie didn't teach again until after his death in 1906. Then she taught a school just east of Sturgis in District 80. The wages were $40.00 per month, and it was a six-month school. Starting in September, 1907, Jessie taught in Lawrence County, the Boulder Park School just west of Sturgis about five miles. This was a five-month school and the salary was $50.00 per month. Jessie rode horseback from Sturgis. At night, she would climb a steep hill, directly adjacent to the north of her little log cabin school, and whistle for her horse. He would come on the run and take her home through Boulder Canyon.
After [Charle's death], Jessie married Roscoe (Rock) Keene. He was a well-known stockman and banker in Meade County who came to South Dakota in 1881, walking most of the way as a hired hand, helping drive a herd of cattle.
Jessie had a homestead on Alkali Divide. They lived in her claim shack until she could prove up on the homestead. She then traded homesteads with Ernest Orr. They then moved to the Alkali Creek OI6 Ranch. After a few years, they moved to Sturgis, and Rock hired men to run the ranch for him.216

Della A. Michaels
1910

"We were not getting ahead, and it looked as if we never would there in Sioux City, where my husband was working in a packing plant." said Mrs. Michaels, commonly know as Grandma. "We started out here in 1910 but I got sick on the way and had to go back so we didn't get her until the following year. We filed on a homestead between Sturgis and Faith and our son, Orel, and I held down the homestead while my husband went back to Sioux City and worked. Our first homestead house was only a dugout. It had one small window in it, and the door opened out so it would give us more room. At first, we didn't even have a stove, and we dug a hole in the ground and used a grate over it until we could get a stove."
"There was an awful blizzard and Orel and I were snowed in. It looked as if we couldn't get out at all, then he thought of crawling through the window and got the snow

shovelled away from the door. That was when we decided the extra room we got from having the door open out didn't pay, so Orel changed the door right away. The dugout was fourteen by sixteen and the first stove we had was one of those little topsy affairs," said Grandma, whose memory is very keen and accurate.

Now she can smile as she recalls once in those times when the pickin's was so slim that the family exchequer had simmered down to a few cents. They talked it over and decided to squander the whole works recklessly on a piece of salt pork. "It wasn't the pork we were after, but the seasoning to make gravy with, as we hardly dared waste the meat by eating it, as long as we could squeeze out more seasoning." She chuckles at those early hardships and is proud that they were able to surmount them.

"Things were tough for me and every once in awhile Orel would say, "Now, when we get the next check from Dad, we're heading back to Sioux City right away." But I figured we had already gone through so much to get hold of the land that far, so I wouldn't give up," said Grandma.

She made her own soap and her own clothes, and water had to be carried quite a distance on the homestead. For laundry use, they hauled it on a sled-like affair called a "stone boat". Fuel posed no problem to her as it was a matter of picking it up on the prairie.

She laughed softly as she recalled some of her bread-making experiences in the early years. The little topsy stove had no oven, so Grandma would set her yeast, nurse it along to a certain stage, then would take it to a neighbor's to bake. The neighbor lived two miles away, but that distance didn't hinder them from being neighbors in those good old days. I had to walk all the way with the bread," Grandma recalled.

It was a hot day when she and the bread started on their way to the neighbor's. It was a race between her and the bread all the way, and it seemed like the faster she would walk, the faster the bread would raise towards the top of the pan. It even threatened to crawl over the sides of the pan and string down on the prairie. For awhile it looked like a losing battle, with the bread and the hot weather winning over Grandma. But her legs were young and sturdy then, and she sped up so she finally managed to beat the bread to the draw.

It was then a simple matter for her to get the fuel to do her baking. This she did by just scampering around the prairie picking up the nice, dry cow chips in her gingham apron. They made a quick fire and good and hot, but they didn't last long, and the neighbor's stove had to be fed constantly while the bread was baking. There was a good excuse to visit a little, while the bread cooled down, so Grandma could carry it home again, no racing needed then.

Life in the dugout for the Michael's family was only a very temporary thing, just as for many of the early pioneers. The second year they bought an old granary and hitched it to the dugout, making another good room. Grandma began to feel real proud and happy about her home and was hopeful for the future.

Although she is a little person, her willing hands never hesitated at any work, no matter how hard. She made a real good hand when she helped her son break up the tough new sod. They needed the sod, which lay in neat chunks along the rows, and Grandma helped carry the big hunks of sod so they could lay it up on the outside of the granary walls. This was called "sodding up" and it bluffed away the cold blasts of winter and acted as a cooling agent in the summer.

Then the Michaels got a break when their daughter and her husband moved out near them. The son-in-law and Orel worked together and could accomplish much more. For five years Michaels worked every winter in Sioux City and returned home in summertime. "Then he managed to get hold of a team and freighted while we held things down on the land. The dog and I herded our cows. While my husband would be worrying about how I was getting along at home, I'd be worrying about how he was doing on the road. You never could tell what might happen. One of the horses might get sick, or the wagon break down. He freighted between Newell and Goldfield, but that little town does not exist now. It was only a post office and a store then," she recalled.

One of the most amusing things that happened to her in the rugged life on the homestead could so easily have cost her life. While it was happening it was not all funny.

"The creek came up after a heavy rain, and we couldn't get across it, but we were out of coffee. I thought I could show my husband I could make it, as he had been putting off the trip, anyway. He saw me starting across the bridge plank, but I soon decided I could make it across by crawling. I had no more than started to crawl when I rolled over and right into the water. My husband called out to me to hang onto a rope and he managed to get me fished out. I started for the house, wet as a drowned rat, and, of course, mad as a wet hen. He followed along behind, laughing. Anyway, he went after the coffee then," said Grandma with a chuckle.

The Michael's determination soon began to pay off, and they accumulated cows and built their herd up to 150 head. They graduated from the dugout and its granary addition and build a good four-room house on their land. Grandma was proud of the accomplishments, and that South Dakota home was one of her dearest possessions.217

Minnie Petersen Meier
Fall River County
1887

A party by the name of E. C. Meyer (better known as Looker Meyer) located my father on the exemption claim where I now live, on Indian Creek. When we first came there, there were quite a few Indians around but they never molested us in any way. We did have an Indian Scare during the winter of 1890 but it was dissipated without much trouble. Women and children went to the Circle Bar Ranch and then went on to Fort Robinson, for protection, until the Indian chief was killed and the uprising ceased to exist.*

Our very first home was a tent pitched in the shade of a tree. One day, a cloud burst with hail came along and our tent was washed away. I nearly drowned before my father rescued me. We learned to live further away from the creek. Indian Creek is nearly seventy-five miles long with a rapid fall and, when swollen, can do a lot of damage. At that time, we had twenty-five chickens. They were all washed away. The rooster took refuge on a log and started crowing as he floated down the stream.

In 1887, shortly after we came to the country, M. J. Gayhart started a store on Hat Creek, not very far from where we lived. This store burned down and he rebuilt it at Montrose where it still stands. Mr. Gayhart was also Justice of the Peace. We would walk over to the Montrose Store every Saturday for our mail and would go to church on Sunday to the same Catholic Church which stands there now. This church was built by my brother-in-law, Mr. Remm, with help of members of the congregation. Mrs. Remm was my husband's sister.

About the time this church was built, Mrs. Remm died during childbirth, leaving him with three small children to care for. Medical help was almost unobtainable. There was no real physician closer than Valentine. People had to depend on older people, who used old-fashioned remedies, for medical attention. In case of childbirth, it was usually a midwife who attended.

In walking to and from the store and church, we had to pass by cattle on the range. These cattle were unfamiliar with people travelling on foot and would sometimes charge us and cause us to take refuge in ditches, ravines or behind rocks.

In 1888, during the winter of the Great Blizzard, we were living in a dug-out. The dug-out became so deeply covered with snow that my sister and I, who were alone at the time, had difficulty in getting out. We were stuck there for about three days. Finally, Dave Andreson, who lived close by, came along on horseback. He helped us clear a path through the snow, and cut some wood. He also gave us a rabbit which he had shot on the way over.

We had many ups and down during the years which followed. In 1888, the year of the great blizzard, we were hit hard. Cattle stood up against trees and froze to death by the hundreds. Following this came drought, and cattle starved to death for want of food.

When we lived in the dug-out we would open burlap sacks and spread them on the floor for a carpet. Sometimes we would put on two or three layers. We would fasten the corners down with wooden pegs to keep them from curling up. When we swept the floor we would dampen it with water to keep the dust down. The walls were white-washed.

We came to Sioux Country in the days of rivalry between the cattlemen and the sheepmen and also at a time when the old settlers, used to the open range, resented the intrusion of newcomers. There were many unpleasant occurrences between the various factions and sometimes even bullets would fly back and forth.

In the early days we had to stake our cow and horse as they would get with the range cattle and the cowboys would run them. They did not want homesteaders to settle in this cattle country because it disturbed their free range. Later, we made a rail fence. In our family, the flat on which it stood is still called Wooden Fence Flat. That was the pasture for our cow and horse. Sometime after this, my father bought another pony and we then had a team of horses to work. People, in general, were quite poor and had to get along with very little.

When I was young, I used to work quite a lot for the neighbors, besides doing farm work of various kinds. I was quite strong and could do this. It helped along financially, even though wages were small.

In those early days, we used candles for light. Most were just braided rags put in a can of tallow. Matches were not plentiful. We would run out of them occasionally and would have to start a fire by pounding rocks together over dry hay until a spark would start. It was common to bank fires so that they would be kept alive indefinitely.

There were a lot of gray wolves in the country during the early nineties. I remember, in 1894 they were especially bad, and horses and cattle were killed in great number. One day, I heard one of our bucket calves bawling and I went out to see what was the matter. I saw a gray wolf close to the house. He had hold of the calf and was killing it. We had a good dog and I called him. He fought the wolf, causing him to let loose of the calf but then the wolf turned on the dog. While they were fighting I turned and went into the house fearing that the wolf would finally attack me. Organized wolf hunts were staged on Sundays. The wolves were hunted down and ultimately they left the country excepting for a few strays.

I lived with my father and mother until 1895 when I was married. After that, my father and mother separated and my childhood home was broken up.

My husband had started to break up his land with ox-team and had built some improvements at the time of our marriage. He bought my father's pre-emption; the original land has been increased to 2180 acres. My husband and I first lived in a dugout. Later we built a log house, and finally the house in which I make my home.

We did all we could do to get enough to eat, ourselves. We hunted buffalo and antelope along the creek. We ate potato pancakes, baked biscuits in a Dutch Oven and used roasted barley for coffee. It finally got so bad that the government had to furnish seed wheat, flour, yeast, salt and dry salt pork for farmers. We finally purchased some chickens and a few cows.

I would make butter and pack it in jars and about every two weeks a neighbor and myself would take it to Dudley (now an addition to Edgemont) and peddle it from house to house for ten to twelve cents a pound. There were no cream separators then, and we had to keep the milk sweet by putting cold water around the cans two or three times a day. We would get up in the morning about four o'clock and make the trip to Dudley, peddle our butter and eggs and return home about midnight. It was about a thirty-eight mile trip one way by trail. Eggs were five cents a dozen.

Of course, we had no automobile in those days. We travelled by team and wagon, although most of the travelling was done by ox-team. When we finally bought a spring-wagon, we thought we were fixed-up right. We had no machinery on the ranch. We cut hay with a scythe, raked it with a homemade rake with wooden pegs for teeth and stacked it with forks made from a forked limb of a tree. We planted corn by hand and cut it with a knife. Clothing was also quite primitive.

A man by the name of Rheinhart used to make wooden shoes out of cottonwood blocks and we would wear them on dress occasions. In winter, we would wrap our feet in gunny sacks and tie them on with cord. Whenever the weather permitted, we would go barefooted. We never went very far away from home because we always had chores to do, morning and night. For work garments, we wore dresses made of overall goods. When we went to church, we had calico dresses, the skirts of which were so long they nearly reached the ground.

Most of the people drove ox teams to church. Later, people came to the country with more money and they traveled in lumber wagons. My father's first team was a white pony and a milk cow.

My life, for the most part, may be said to be fairly happy and yet a few clouds have passed across my horizon. My sister, Anna, drowned in a small creek by our place in June, 1891. Her death left me very lonely for a while. Our son, John, died in 1903. My husband died in 1934. I have seen many of my friends and neighbors laid away during the years I have lived near Ardmore.

In reminiscing, I can look back over many incidents and happenings which worried and bothered me at the time, but time has softened their harshness and some of them seem rather amusing in the light of memory.

We have come quite a long way since the dug-out days. Our home now consists of eight rooms with running water and electric lights. My son and his family live with me on the original place. His children represent the fourth generation, from the time it was taken as a homestead. Whatever prosperity and accumulation of property we have made has come through hard work, economical living and family cooperation.

There are days and times that I would not care to live over again, but on the whole, life for me has been, perhaps, more happy than the average. As the beautiful colors of evening begin to show in the West, I find considerable satisfaction in what has been accomplished, in the friends who have made the road easier as I have traveled along, in the children who have come to bless our home and who have stood by me through the years, and in the blessings I have enjoyed as I have journeyed thus far through life.218

Amelia J. Miller
Lawrence County
1887

When the Sidney stage coach crept up the hill into Lead one day back in 1883, straining under the load of a mother and her nine children, her two servants, and baggage for all (behind a string of six horses and six mules), the citizens of that gold rush community thought a circus was coming to town.

As they gathered around the coach staring at the high silk hats and swallow-tailed coats and wondering what sort of a performance this troupe was going to put on for them, a man named Harry Sleep stepped up and said, "That's not a circus, that's my family from England!"

That was how Mrs. Amelia J. Miller of Spearfish was introduced to the Black Hills and their colorful citizens. Now seventy-three-years-old and the mother of seven children of her own, she has found that pioneering in the early days wasn't a circus, either.

She was just a little girl of eleven years when she first greeted her father on the streets of Lead. Harry Sleep had preceded them to the Black Hills two years previous, drawn by the fabulous stories that gold was to be had by the bushel and all you had to do was pick it up and struggle away with it. Disillusioned, he applied for a job at the Homestake Mine and was hired as the company's first watchman.

"The trip over here from London was by boat that had some kind of a tarp sail-top and followed the wind, although they tried to guide such boats by poles, not at all like our boats these days," said the little lady.

The long trip across the ocean was tiresome and the whole family sat down on the ground to rest when they landed in the United States. It seemed good to have their feet on land.

Mrs. Miller says it was like riding into a cow corral when she first went through Rapid City as the "town" was no more than a wide spot in the road. "Spearfish had no sidewalks, not even board ones, and the town was only a little huddle of houses with only one hotel -- that was the Queen City which is still standing."

"Father homesteaded and founded a ranch near Crow Peak where we lived for some time," said Mrs. Miller. "I recall they washed gold out of the creeks by hand at that time. I had never been out of London until we left there to come to the United States.

Mrs. Miller says it was difficult for her mother to adjust herself from the soft city life of England to that of a pioneer. "She had never done a tap of work for herself in all her life. That had all been done by servants and maids," Mrs. Miller said.

"She insisted that all my brothers continue to wear the silk top hats and swallow-tail coats. One day, when one of them came home with the rim of the precious hat around his neck like a necktie, mother just sat down and cried. 'There isn't another one this side of London,' she moaned." "I warned you fellows," Mrs. Miller's father had said, "that if you wore those monkey hats around this town someone would make a necktie out of them for you."

"Then," Mrs. Miller continued, "when my brother came home with, according to mother, 'one of those awful felt hats,' to replace the silk top hat, mother sat down and cried again. 'You look just like all these other bums now,' she wailed." As time passed, she had to get used to the change in her children as they grew from the pampered children of an England household to stalwart pioneers of Dakota Territory.

Soon after arriving in the Black Hills, Mrs. Miller moved with her mother and the rest of the family to a farm fifteen miles west of Spearfish.

"It wasn't easy in those days, scraping a living from the soil," she said. "We hadn't many conveniences. I recall the first threshing machine I ever saw, it was a steam engine pulled by oxen."

"I remember how we used to haul wood from the nearby hills by ox team to feed the firebox of the steamer. Then we had to have another team of horses to carry water to the engine to make the steam."

"The second year we were there, though, we didn't have to worry about threshing. The golden wheat was this high," she said as she held her slim hand up to her shoulder. "Some of the boys had gone to Whitewood to get a binder. When they came home the golden harvest had been pounded into the ground by a hailstorm."

"Then there was the fire. I was still just a girl when one cold January night our house burned to the ground, driving us out into the snow with only our night clothes on. I froze my feet that time. We had no equipment to fight fires with then so we just watched it burn."

"What about forest fires in the summer?" she was asked. "Oh, we just let them burn out, too. There weren't enough people in those days to fight them. As a protection to our property we used to plow fireguards around our land as far back in the hills as we could get."

"And the Indians?" "We never had any trouble with them. They used to come in our place often. We found if we treated them as equals and were fair with them they became very friendly."

Dancing was a favored entertainment in those days and at a dance the young English girl met Joe Miller, "a strapping six-footer." The first thing she knew, she was "switching her name to his" when she was only seventeen-years-old.

The young couple continued pioneering as they took a homestead a few miles from the Wyoming line and moved there to make a home. But this little pioneer lady was spared many hardships and inconveniences as they managed to build a commodious house on their land.

"I could stand on my front porch and see deer almost anytime. They looked so nice running in the woods that I always hated the idea of eating the venison. There was no hunting license required so we had plenty of wild meat all the time.

"I had never even seen a cow until we came to the United States because I had always lived in London. The first cow I saw seemed like such a funny-looking animal," said Grandma with a chuckle. "But, I soon got so I could milk just as fast as anybody. We proved up on our land and lived there many years. Our six boys and one girl were brought up on the ranch until it came time to finish their education and then we moved into Spearfish."

Mrs. Miller is a small woman. She doesn't look as though she ever had been capable physically of working in the fields, "but I've done it many a time," she said. "Joe, that's my husband, died when our oldest son was only fifteen years old. With seven children, I had to get out and work." Mr. Miller's death was the result of an accident that happened years before, when a stick of dynamite exploded in his hand, shattering his arm to the shoulder.

Six years ago Mrs. Miller left the ranch and moved to Spearfish. She treasures a "brooch" pin made sixty years ago from gold that her father took out of the ground. The pin has a cameo setting. But the thing this gentle little lady seems to treasure most is the stove!

Nobody can say how old the stove is and it probably came into the Hills by ox team. It is the round, oak type with an urn top which indicates it is a pioneer. The stove is taller than Grandma. "Somebody is everlastingly trying to buy this old stove from me. They want it for a garbage burner or something else. I always tell them nothing doing, I'm using it myself, and it comes in handy."

When she was asked if she had ever wanted to go back to England she was quick to answer: "No, it seemed there was so much to see and do over here. Now in London, for instance, we hardly ever saw a horse and here in the Black Hills we soon learned to handle horses and ride horseback. We always liked that."

It was evident that she still possesses the old pioneer spirit and determination that carried her through the difficult times. Last week she fell in her home and injured her back. Though only able to move about with difficulty, she hasn't allowed the injury to confine her to bed. "I've been through so much," she said, "one more thing hadn't ought to matter."219

"Happy Memories"
Mary Doody Mochon
Lawrence County
1879

My first memory was when I passed Fort Meade, July 10, 1879. The soldiers were camped at the foot of Bear Butte, on the east side. There was a village of white canvas tents. Later, Fort Meade was built. The memory of these white tents still lingers on with me. The village was on the left. I was two-years-and-four-months old.

My father, James Doody, was born on a farm near Rickeleau river, Quebec, Canada. One of nine boys and one girl, his father came from Ireland and filed on land. His mother, Marie Treudeau, came from France. They were married in Canada. As a youth, my father went apprentice to a carriage builder, and later had a factory of his own.

My mother, Delia Marie, was the first child of Frances Goyette and Onisim Martell Goyette. Frances Goyette was a fisherman, he owned dories and with one brother caught fish to sell. When he had made enough money, he bought a farm and built a brick house on his farm near the village of St. Atenas in Quebec, Canada.

I was born March 24, 1877. When two weeks old, my father and his brother decided to leave their factory, (building wagons, buggies, sleighs and cutters) to another brother and come to the Black Hills. Grand stories of placer mining on Gold Run Creek had reached even the village of St. Atenas.

On the way over, a smooth salesman talked my father into buying a pick and shovel for ten dollars, telling him there were none to be had in Deadwood. Father often told this story, which was a lesson to him, never buy anything not needed at the time. He never used the pick and shovel for mining. When he arrived in Deadwood he found out that rich land could be had for filing. He immediately took out citizen papers and filed on a farm near Red Water River.

My father soon had rich native hay, which he cut and hauled to Deadwood with oxen team and walked all the way. If he got on the load of hay, he said the oxen would stop and lie down. The first summer, he broke land for farming, started to raise cattle, and he built a frame house. Two years later he sent for my mother to come.

Mother boarded the train in Montreal, Canada, with two children who had whooping cough. She said that the second day of travel the children stopped coughing, caused by the change of climate. The railroad went as far as Fort Pierre; then the three of us came on the Deadwood stagecoach, two mounted soldiers riding on each side of the coach for protection from the Indians. My father met us where the soldiers were camped at the foot of Bear Butte, then drove his team of horses to his ranch on Red Water. That is the only remembrance of my trip, when I was with father and mother going to Red Water. Mother liked the place.

Father had a big black dog, Rover. I would sit on a gunny sack and the dog would take hold of a corner and drag me down the incline from the house. I remember it was fun. My brother had a pocket knife and he got a leather strap he wanted to split in two. He asked me to take hold of one end. Taking his knife, he cut towards me. The knife slipped and cut my finger which was bleeding very much. I remember taking a large pan to have blood drip in, like I had seen saving blood when butchering hogs. I was surprised that only a few drops were in the pan when I expected to half-fill the pan.

My father never drank or smoked. He was a quiet, unassuming man, a deep thinker which brought him success. In the evening he would tell us stories about Indians, which he made up. My father's policy was, go to bed early and get up early, which I have kept up to this day.

My mother said, "Why don't you make Mary a cabriolet (small wagon)?" This toy was very nice and I enjoyed it, large enough to sit in, but a bit heavy to wheel around, especially when full of odds and ends like children do.

Most all small children seem to want to do things they should not. As a child I, too, had that impish impulse. Anything for a laugh. Laughing, like tears, comes easy in childhood.

We lived near a large river where we could go in swimming at will, often many times a day. There was one place forbidden, because the bottom was covered with slate and some places, the water quite deep for children. Our gang would form a chain by holding hands and walk through this deep spot. The bravest one would lead and walk until the water was over his head. By the time he was out, the middle one would be under, so on until the last one was safely out. We figured if one fell, the others would pull him or her out. Fortunately, none of us fell or I am afraid our parents would have found the gang under water.

At another time it was bitter cold. I wanted to try the ice. The gang figured, if it will hold the biggest one, it would hold all the others and would be safe for skating. I walked out over thin ice and fell in. The water came up to my waist. That stopped the fun for the day. Everyone was trying to wring out the icy water from my clothes. We did not want to go in the house for fear of being scolded. After a long time trying to dry my clothes in the sun, my mother called us. When mother called, we came, no matter what had happened. The story had to be told. Mother made me put on dry clothes and I was none the worse for my experience.

One day the gang found a turtle by the river. We took sticks to touch the head. The turtle bit and held onto one of the sticks. The bravest one of us took hold of the tail and we carried the turtle in the house and let it loose. When it began to run across the floor, two of the mothers who were there, jumped on chairs and screamed. We had our laugh and then tears. The turtle was taken outdoors and the head cut off, cleaned, and turtle soup we ate. For a long time the head would snap at a stick. After a day or two, a stick would not rouse the head to snap. One of the girls picked it up and it snapped her finger. How she shook her hand and screamed! I still get a chuckle over the recollection.

One morning we children found a skunk in the front yard with its head in a discarded can of salmon. No doubt it had been trying all night to remove the can. We took sticks and, by coaxing and leading, we managed to drive the very polite animal to the river bank, which skunk fell in the water. There appeared a circle of oil the color of the rainbow, but of the skunk variety. It may have calmed the water, but alas, did not remove the can. The little black-and-white animal drown.

My mother, Delia, was a very pretty woman with light brown hair, very curly, and brown eyes. She was very quick and capable, a born teacher. Although she never taught in public schools, mother was forever teaching: reading, writing, arithmetic, sewing, knitting and crochet, how to bake and keep house, to her children and all those who wanted to learn. My mother taught me prayers and catechism. At night before going to bed, each one of us came to kneel at her knee and say our prayers, until we, the five of us children, learned them by heart. The Lords Prayer, The Angelic Salutation, The Apostles Creed, The Confiteor, The Act of Contrition, The Acts of Faith, Hope and Charity, the Ten Commandments, and many other prayers.

After father's cattle were too many for the farm on Red Water, he drove the herd to the range in Wyoming, sold the farm and came to St. Onge. He bought the home place and had the deed made in my mother's name.

Mother gave one acre of land on the best corner of the home farm for a Catholic church. Then mother, with horse and buggy, went around the community subscribing for money and time to build a Catholic church. Within the year the church was ready to be dedicated, and mass was celebrated once a month. On other Sundays I taught a class of children the catechism and prayers. While the church was being built the mass was celebrated in our living room.

My mother learned to read and write in English and learned the English language. When she came to Dakota she did not know a word of English. She knew French and could read Latin.

I learned to read, write and cipher (by private tutor) in French. I was ten-and-a-half years old when I entered public school. I learned the English language and graduated from the eighth grade in six years. I had a teacher who wanted to learn French. I brought him a French grammar and taught him. He learned to read and write and talk fairly good French. Then my uncle wanted to learn to read and write English. I used my school books and taught him. He learned he could speak English, all that being done after school hours.

On January 27, 1897, in the Catholic church in St. Onge (the one on my mother's farm) I was married to a man of my nationality, Oliva Joseph Mochon. He brought me to Lead on the same day to a new four-room house, which he had furnished. For my part I had a very well-filled hope chest of bed linens and table linens. With eighteen, full-size bed sheets, pillow cases, and all in keeping, blankets, quilts, towels, etc., we started housekeeping and were happy. I kept the house immaculate. O.J. liked to eat and I liked to cook.

I was near a good library and made use of it, read all the books to give me more knowledge, then went to night school and learned a business course which I used to help my husband in his store.

The teacher I taught French to, gave me a good start in Art and Drawing. He said that Art and Music should be taught in all schools. Many years later his wish came true, as Music and Art are now taught in all accredited schools.

I took painting lessons in china. I learned fast and soon had my own studio and a class teaching painting, also took orders to paint dishes. With the money from the lessons I bought a kiln and did firing.

For recreation, we went to stage shows in the Miners Union Opera House. Both liked the same shows and the same music and dancing. Grand Balls were given by different organizations. Dancing would start at nine o'clock to midnight and then to a big supper, return to dance until four o'clock, which was hard for men who went to work at six o'clock in the morning.

Then the Midnight Dancing Club was organized by the young married people. Dancing was from nine to midnight, much better for those who had to work early. This club was formal. I remember dancing with a dress that had a long train. I had to pick up and hold the train while dancing, and drop it to let it sweep going to our seat. The couple walking back had to be careful not to step on the train. Later it became the fashion for the ladies to carry a sheaf of flowers to the dance, place the flowers on our chair to get up and dance, then pick them up on returning.

We belonged to the Bon Ton Card club and played cards once a month. A dancing school started in Lead, teaching the new steps by a professor. O.J. and I would go on Saturday nights and learn the new steps: the Baltimore, Sylvan Glide, Two-Step, Scottish, and the ever popular Waltz.

After four-and-a-half years, our son was born. He was the prettiest baby, plump and fair, with large brown eyes and blond, curly hair. The moment my baby was placed into my arms is the happiest memory. Then my life was very full and so happy with our little son. He never caused me any worries.

When our son left for college, the days were endless. Then I decided to learn Spanish, went two years to the regular class, all that was taught in the school in Lead, then subscribed for a Spanish paper. I can now speak, read and write French, English, and Spanish, learned in the order given. 220

Minerva Ellen Morris and Minnie Williamson, sisters
Lawrence County
1883

Through the lighted window, Minerva Ellen Morris, ninety-seven, looked like the painting of Whistler's mother as she sat in a rocker, erect and dainty, with thick, dark-gray hair framing her face like a cap.

Mrs. Morris, of Spearfish, will celebrate her ninety-eighth birthday next March, and her sister, Mrs. Minnie Williamson, will be ninety on her next birthday.

"We came to Spearfish from Missouri," Mrs. Morris said. "I was born in Ohio, but we moved to Iowa, which was a new country, when I was a little girl. After I married, we went to Missouri. Exciting happenings? I don't remember many; we just came by covered wagons -- no excitement."

"What did we eat? Why, we had plenty of everything; we carried flour, bacon and other staples. I used to bake pancakes. I made a lot of pies too. We had a stove which my husband used to take out and set up. There were lots of berries along the way."

Here Mrs. Morris chuckled, "Once I baked a gooseberry pie and set it on the grub box to cool. I forgot to put it inside, and the rough riding made it slide out of the wagon. The folks coming behind us had part of a fresh pie! We used to buy butter from the farmers along the way. Once, when a girl from our party inquired about butter, she turned away from the door and called, 'Drive on, Dad! Butter's fifty cents a pound, and made by a man!'"

"We arrived in Spearfish in 1883, and my husband's first job was to help build the Congregational church. He also hauled the first load of stone for the Spearfish Normal school. For years, Bud (John, his name was) helped furnish the music for the dances, too."

Mrs. Morris recalls the time the Thoen Stone* was found and the speculation on how it came there. She also lived in Spearfish when the lynching of Harry Tuthill took place.

"That was awful! He was wounded and captured when the Exelbee horse-thief gang had a brush with the law. He was taken out of bed, here in Spearfish, and hanged. My boy went down and saw him hanging in a tree by the creek."

Another murder victim was a woman. "She didn't amount to much, I guess. The man who killed her walked into the store beforehand and bought the cartridges. He said to the folks in the store. 'I'm inviting you all to a first-class funeral'; then he went out and shot her. What happened to him? Why, he just got on his horse and rode out of town."
 Cowboys used to ride in and shoot up the town, Mrs. Morris said. She remembers her neighbors telling how the bullets from some happy puncher's gun zinged across their table at dinner time.
 "There were some Indian scares, but no trouble. One family left and went back East because they were afraid of the Indians. When we were living on the Deadwood road, we saw a bunch of Indians being taken to a reservation by some soldiers." Again her eyes twinkled, "I still can see these Indian women walking in the mud, and the dogs riding in the wagons!"

Minnie Williamson
 Although Mrs. Minnie Williamson will soon be ninety, she says she feels about sixty-five. She loves to walk, and frequently hikes more than a mile a day. She also does the work in the apartment she shares with her sister.
 "Perhaps it's my Irish ancestry that makes me so spry" she commented. "I've never weighed over eighty-five pounds in my life. Our family has always had good health."
 Before her marriage, Mrs. Williamson taught school in Iowa. "If some of the same methods were still used today, children would be better-taught. Too often they seem to get a little of this and a little of that. When we taught a process, we also taught the reason for using it."
 Minnie Williamson helped to start one of the first Sunshine Clubs there. The club had fourteen members and was called "In As Much".
 "We used to go down to the courthouse and get the names of poor people who needed help," she said. "Doing something for somebody else is one of the grandest feelings in the world!"221

Maude D. Ogden
Lawrence County
1877

I was the second daughter of William McK. Dennee and Helen Davy, born October 18, 1866, in Bath, Ontario, in a beautiful old home with fireplaces to heat it, and candles and lamps for light, and brass doorknobs of lion heads to be polished.

Our father came to the Black Hills in 1876, and my mother, with the two daughters, in 1877, in the month of May. Taking passage at Ft. Pierre, we were given the front seat and the nine other passengers, all men, filled the wagon. They were all Tenderfeet! Because of the heavy rains, the new coach could not take the trip. The roads were full of gumbo, so an ox wagon was substituted with a canvas cover. It was a trying and difficult trip of ten days across a new prairie country. The front wagon bow was broken, so the canvas was pulled down tight and held in place by the driver. I remember my mother sitting very straight, wearing a fashionable, little, black, spring hat perched on her head, which was constantly being knocked off at the jolting of the wagon, and the pulling of the heavy, wet canvas over us. My mother was a sweet, dignified, aristocratic woman, and the trip must have been very trying.

We were told there was a good hotel at Cheyenne River which we reached late on a dark, rainy night. There was much shouting and calling, and presently lights showed, and we were sure we saw them in the upper windows of the hotel. The river was a raging torrent, so directions on how, and where to cross, were shouted to us. The lights we saw, were lanterns showing the way to the river, and where to cross. The men in the wagon were ordered out, and they helped to keep the floating wagon from going downstream, while the four horses plunged and lunged, but finally reached footing on the opposite bank. We were comforted with the hopes of a good meal and bed.

The hotel proved to be a big tent where we were given one corner with blankets on the ground. The men sprawled all over, and at the rear, horses were tied and fed, champing and stamping all night.

We did have a sort of hotel at a station called Crook City, now a ghost town about a mile from Whitewood. We had beds. They were divided by curtains hung on wires. Once they fell down, and there was much shouting. It took us nearly all day to reach the mining town of Deadwood.

My parents were hospitable people who contributed to those less fortunate and in trouble. My mother cared for many sick. The first Episcopalian clergyman was taken ill and brought to our house and cared for, till he returned back East. A well-known, cultured gentleman was a guest during a severe illness; he had come out for fortune and adventure. The banker's family, good friends of ours, lost their two little boys with diphtheria, and after their death, they visited us till their house was built. Many families were cared for by my parents, for we had plenty. Not long ago, I received a letter from Rhode Island telling me how her family had been befriended -- referring to the time they were without means, and destitute for food, and were grateful for assistance. They are now a wealthy family.

I was shielded from the rough, western life, but remember being accosted on Main Street by Calamity Jane, who asked "What is your name, little girl?" After a brief conversation, she took me by the hand, and said "Here, you give this little girl some candy." I knew she was not considered a very nice lady.

Another time stamped on my memory was being taken to a corral where several Indians were camping with their horses in the lower part of Deadwood, and were here as witnesses in a murder trial. The Lakota men gathered around my good friend, Col. Donnan, a newspaperman, and he called their attention to my long braid of hair. Lifting it up, he asked the interpreter how Sitting Bull would like that. I was a bit nervous, but they all laughed and shook hands and said "How."

At a service conducted by an Episcopal layman, and held in the one decent theatre, one hundred men were in attendance, and my mother played the piano. I can remember, that Sunday night, how their voices rang out as they joined in "Nearer My God to Thee". Strange to say, Sunday was the only night there was not a performance in the theatre. Shortly after this, my mother, with two other fine women, organized a society to raise funds to start the Episcopal Church.222

Mrs. J. N. Gorum
Deadwood, South Dakota

May Edna Painter
Pennington County
1881

What do we mean when we say Pioneer Woman? Resourcefulness without age. Character that never cracked under pressure. One knew that May Painter would be in control of herself and her section of the situation whether it be a visit of a drunken Indian to her isolated home in the range country in the early 1900's or an atomic attack from over the Polar cap enroute to Ellsworth Base. These are the qualities of the pioneer woman; these were the qualities of May Painter.

We see the pioneer woman as a teacher as well as a home builder and trainer of children. This, too, was May Painter. The daughter of pioneers, she and her two sisters were taught at their mother's knee and were sent to the Normal at Spearfish for training as teachers. They taught country schools of the area, where their work included adult education as well as schoolroom teaching. Community building and responsibility were instilled in these young women.

May Painter was always a teacher -- her marriage but centering her efforts in her own children. And, like a teacher, she never stopped learning, feeling even in her seventies and eighties that she must learn and pass on to others what she had learned.223

You can't find Grandma Painter at home on the U T Ranch in Belle Fourche, these days. The eighty-three-year-old retired school-teacher is zooming over Mexico to visit Acapulco and Yacatan. Though while she is "way up there in the sky between airfields," all she can see "is the back-end of a lot of clouds," she isn't missing a thing.

The airplane is a far cry from the early days in 1880 when Grandma rocked over the hills of South Dakota in a covered wagon. Mrs. Lewis Levi Painter of Belle Fourche was just a little girl when her parents and the family started their wagon trek out of Council Bluffs headed for the Black Hills and perhaps, California.

Indians

"We had a lot of funny experiences with the Indians," said Mrs. Painter. "It was quite different from the reception given white people only two years before. They lost their scalps."

"At one point on our trip northwest, mother discovered a leak in the canvas covering our wagon, and the rain was dripping into our cracker supply. Afraid the whole batch would be spoiled if she let one mildewed cracker remain, she told us to throw the damaged ones out of the wagon."

"It was fun for the youngsters, but the Indian women were puzzled by such wasteful behavior. They kept muttering, 'bad child,' in their language and scooped up the crackers as fast as they could, stuffing them inside their gray blankets."

The family's pet Newfoundland dog failed to return to the family wagon one night. Early the next day, Indians appeared and offered to sell the dog to them. In the background, Indian women protested the goings-on and snatches of their conversation were translated to their children. "Making soup" and "black, curly moccasins" with suggestive looks at the poor dog that terrified the children. Finally, their father and the lead Indian struck a bargain and the dog was left with them.

The pioneer family passed through "fire and flood", literally, on its wagon trip to the Northwest. Because of the early snow, they stayed in Hagen's Bend -- about twenty miles from Yankton -- and it was here that the water from the upper Missouri flooded the frontier settlement.

For days, the family of five lived on the top of their upturned wagon box in the log cabin, waiting for the water to go down or freeze solidly enough so they could move to a house on higher ground. There wasn't a boat within twenty miles. The men of the settlement inched their way on planks over the thin ice to Gayville, the nearest town, to secure food supplies. Grandma's family lost all its clothes in the flood, and they called themselves fortunate, still, to escape with their lives, their faithful black iron cookstove, and their wagon.

The day they rolled into Deadwood, the news of President Garfield's assassination was on everyone's tongue. That was July 8, 1881.

Deadwood Fire

The terrible fire which leveled the Fountain City half of Deadwood in fifteen minutes will never be forgotten by Grandma Painter. Those early houses were built of raw pine. The wood was so new, you could see the pitch oozing out of the wood on a hot summer afternoon.

To try to save the wagon, Grandpa set it out in the middle of the street and placed the black cookstove close by. It was the same stove which survived the Hagen's Bend flood the year before.

They had only minutes to act. Down at the local hotel, panic-stricken people threw mirrors out of windows and carried feather beds tenderly down over the stairs. Someone tossed a what-not and a sugar bowl into the Painter wagon during the excitement.

When the fire smoldered down, the little family had again lost all its clothing, but the saddest thing was the loss of their leather-covered books. They could never be replaced.

Grandma Painter's father was a teacher of music, writing and drawing, and in appearance, he resembled a preacher. He was a tall, rangy man with a mustache and beard.

When he taught music, he used a tuning fork, pulling it from between his front teeth to make it sound. The only time Grandma Painter has seen a tuning fork used since, was in Washington, D.C., after one of her flights, when a Russian chorus of fifty was warming up.

"Calamity Jane called on me one day, but I didn't recognize her by the name of Jane Burke," says Grandma Painter. "I was home alone at the time when a lady drove up and asked to camp by the spring. We visited back and forth, and I thought she was a wonderful, kindly person. Later I found out she was the famous Calamity."

One of the best shows on earth to Grandma Painter's thinking, was the eight, matched bays or eight, black horses rushing the big stagecoach out of town every night with a load of gold bullion from the Homestake Mine. There were periodic holdups on the fringe of town and the children used to watch, pop-eyed, while the stage careened by.

"Riding the wild burros over fields in the moonlight was one of the greatest pastimes we children ever had." Miners had left those burros to roam a few years before.

During the years Grandma has lived in South Dakota, she has picked up many Indian words, and can still repeat the first words she heard an Indian say when the little caravan got ready to cross the Crow Creek. 224

PENNINGTON

Alice Dinnis Ham
1882

Living on a ranch was a new experience to mother, but she had been born with two attributes of character which helped her over many hard places; namely, a keen sense of humor and a great love of people. Then too, she had wonderful powers of adaptability.

I think in these years she acquired a great respect and liking for the masculine sex. This remained with her all through the years. After her death, among her dearest possessions, we found a picture of her minister and one of Winston Churchill. This liking for men was, no doubt, acquired during the years when she spent so many months without seeing a woman. At one time, mother didn't set eyes on a woman for six months. Mother was always respected and admired by the men with whom she came in contact, and it spoke well for the chivalry of Western men that she respect them so much.

During these early years, the people who came to our house were a varied crew -- hired men of all grades of intelligence and cleanliness, remittance men from England, Indians, men who had married Indian wives, a notorious woman ox-team driver, a millionaire who had business interests in the West, school teachers, and ministers. By ministers, I mean the Methodist circuit riders. Such is a cross section of the visitors who came to our home.

As was true of so many ranches in those early days, we had seldom, or never, a garden. Sometimes, we were able to buy vegetables from our neighbors. Dairy products were also very scarce. As a child, I can remember the butter disappearing before it got around to me. My father for many years ran a horse ranch. Naturally, milk cows were out of place here.

I have heard mother tell about taking the children to a neighbor's house during an Indian scare. She said she never saw an Indian, but she brought the children home with scarlet fever.

Mother had brought some nice china with her to the ranch. Piece by piece it was broken. Each time, the pieces were picked up with tears. Once, when my older brother had broken several dishes, she wept aloud. My brother said, in horror, "Oh mother, don't cry. You look like a town lady."

My mother was a charter member of the W.C.T.U. at Rapid City. Albeit, she was never a prudish person. I can remember hearing her tell with a chuckle about a neighbor who, when he was drinking, would come to her and cry, and tell his troubles.

In the very early days, one of our neighbors was a wine-bibbing Englishman. He made potent liquor out of wild fruits. One day, in a virtuous mood, he told mother he had stopped drinking and asked her to come and empty out his wine. This she did with dispatch. But soon, the Englishman got a terrible thirst. Angrily, he said to my mother, "Why did you empty my wine? You knew I didn't mean it when I asked you to empty it." Mother only smiled.

Mother was for so many years a rancher's wife. And yet she never milked a cow, rode a horse (only once) or drove a team. There was always a man willing -- nay flattered -- to do these things for her.

In spite of her gayety and kindness, mother was a person of great discernment and determination. Many causes as well as persons have profited by her sponsoring hand. And occasionally, someone has received from her a well-deserved rebuke.225

Mae Florence Spruling Letteer Hudson
1900

She came to visit and be with an aunt while the men were away from home putting up hay, which was not too plentiful that year. Mr. Mattice met her in Pierre. She came by train to Pierre. They crossed the Missouri river by boat. The trip to the ranch was made by lumber wagon, a distance of about seventy miles. He and a neighbor came together, each having a wagon to take home provisions.

There were two stops on the way out: the Hayes store, which was run by Bill Hopkins, and an eating place run by Mrs. Porterfield. (Hayes, of course, is still in existence, only in a little different location.) It was here that she met a cowboy, Henry Hudson. As they were on their way home he was on his way to Pierre. Little did she realize then that South Dakota would be her future home, as she only figured on staying two months. The rest of her life was spent in South Dakota, only going back to Iowa for visits.

Their first date was Thanksgiving. They went to Pedro to a dance, a distance of about fifty miles by team and buggy. It was her first dance. It look a day to go and a day to come home. Many times the dances lasted all night and some of the people would have breakfast before they started home.

While she was visiting, she was doing some sewing for Mrs. Benthine at Leslie. One day Narcissie Narcellehis, a French-Indian who was a good friend of Henry's, said, "Think, says I, if you'll marry the Henry Hudson I'll give you a cow, a calf, a hen and a rooster." She told him she'd ask him. The next day he came and said it had to be by the 15th of February. They were married February 14th, 1901, in Fort Pierre. The day they were married the minister said he had had a very good day; his son was born, two weddings and cleaned his chimney.

To go back to mother's early life, she attended school at Conway, Iowa, and at an early age learned the dressmaker's trade from an aunt, Clare Campbell, who was a seamstress. This being the case I had very few, if any, bought clothes, and can remember how I used to wish for clothes like the other girls, but can see now mine were better.

Their first home was close to Leslie, one of the earliest post offices in that area, on the south side of the Cheyenne River across from the Cherry Creek Agency. Neighbors were few and far between, but their latchstring was always open. Their home was a gathering place for the homesteaders and cowboys as had worked on the roundup.

I can remember her telling how, when there was a big crowd around, they used to play cards to see who would do the dishes -- sometimes the winners -- sometimes the loosers. Our home was always known for its warm hospitality. The Indians came to visit, too. Dad could speak some Sioux, mother couldn't, but got so she could understand some and they could, her.

One day an Indian couple came to visit. Mother noticed the little kids running in and out all the time. After they left she went to put her bread in the oven, which she had raising on the warming oven. Her bread was gone, these little kids had eaten it all.

We always looked forward to the winter holidays, as we always went to a neighbor's or had company, even though we did have to go by team and buggy, or bobsled, if the snow was too deep for the buggy. Mother was a very good cook and was always able to have a good meal from so little. Things we had only on holidays, then, are everyday courses now -- like sweet potatoes, celery, jello, bananas, and oranges.

The folks always had parties or dances at home for the community; usually there was only standing room. The ladies brought sandwiches or cake for lunch; it was passed out free. The music was usually a violin and a piano, they would pass the hat to take up a collection for the music.

School was a problem then, too. The boys went to school at first at Leslie. Then later on in the fall, mother would move to town for the school term. 226

Ella Teed Richards
Butte County
1880

Two sons share memories of their mother.

Joseph Richards writes:
She went to the Black Hills in 1880, going to Bismarck by train. From there she went on to the Hills by stagecoach with out-riders for protection against Indians and highwaymen. She was married on the day of her arrival in Deadwood, to Wyman C. Richards. I, their first child, was born in April, 1881. My father homesteaded, in about 1884, on the Belle Fourche River, in what is now Butte County.

I remember living there when I was four years old, in a two-room log cabin with a dirt floor. Later, my father filed an additional claim, a pre-emption of 160 acres. My mother held down the claim while my father taught school in Central City, about two miles north of Deadwood, until final proof could be made. My father was the second county superintendent of schools in Butte County. Butte County, at that time, included what is now Harding County and Perkins County. Both my parents taught at country schools in the area after moving to the valley.

I remember very distinctly a morning of the spring when I was thirteen, that my mother, up before the rest of us on a Sunday morning, went out for chips with which to kindle the fire. She found a gray wolf sleeping by the chopping block. She went toward him flopping her apron and saying, "shoo, shoo". He did not "shoo" so she went back and picked up a stick. At that, he got up and moved off, in no haste, along the two-wire fence until he came to a place he could crawl under without bending his back too much. "Well, why didn't you call Papa and he might have shot it?" "Oh, I just didn't think of it. I wanted some chips and he was in my way."

She lived to be ninety-two and died at the home of her youngest son. She bore four sons.227

Another son, Harry Richards, tells this story of his mother:
It was while we were living there, that, when my father was late getting home from some trip one evening, my mother

went out and rounded up some wild range cows, under the impression she was bringing home our cows. She brought them home, all right, and put them in the corral, but she wondered whatever had got into those cows to make them act so wild. And when she went out to give them some potato peelings, she found them more scared of her afoot than on horseback. In fact, she decided to leave the milking until Father came home. When he came, he turned them loose, and told her they were not the right cows.

She had a little Indian pony named Topsy with which she got around quite a lot. She rode on a side-saddle with me in her arms and my brother, Joe, five years older, behind the saddle, when my father was away. Some of the time, he was teaching in the Hills while we were holding down the homestead. At other times, one or both taught in neighboring schools. If both taught, there had to be a hired man. They received thirty dollars a month each for teaching, out of which they paid the hired man twenty. That left them twenty a month each but the hired man did not have to use any of his for groceries.

We lived by the Belle Fourche River, a beautiful stream until it was spoiled by mill-tailings brought down by the Whitewood Creek from the stamp mills in the Hills. We had to cross the river to get to Vale or any of the Hills towns. The river had good fords, but in times of high water, or toward spring when the ice was breaking up, we simply had to stay on our own side, sometimes several weeks at a time. At such times there was quite a lot of borrowing back and forth in the neighborhood, mostly of sugar and coffee, I think. I also remember Mother using parched corn as a coffee substitute. There were no bridges until many years later.

We lived in a combination log and frame house of three rooms. In my earliest recollections of it, there was an opening in the kitchen floor down into the cellar and no screen on the door. One day in late summer, my father was helping a neighbor thresh, and my brother was with him, so Mother and I were alone. Our rooster and a few hens had strolled into the kitchen and soon went into the living room when we heard the rooster making the queerest noises. I went out to see what it was all about, and there on the floor by the cellar opening was a good-sized rattlesnake. When I told mother, she took one look at the snake and then went outdoors and got a rock about the size of my head, it seems to me, and threw it at the snake. It missed the snake but completely wrecked a gallon can of kerosene for our lamps, that was sitting nearby. Father had carried it home from Vale on horseback a few days before.

Two or three days later my brother and I, while playing outdoors, found a rattlesnake under an outbuilding. Into the house we ran as fast as we could by way of the kitchen door, to tell Mother. She came at once and when she neared the kitchen door, there lay another snake which we must have missed by two or three inches only, as we ran in barefooted. I think Mother and brother Joe dispatched both of them but I remember that they had quite a time with the one under the outbuilding, Mother finally using her revolver on him.

There were no autos in those days but occasionally there were very bad runaways with the teams, though no one in our family ever got badly hurt. I was in one with Mother and some guests from the town of Whitewood. One morning we started for Whitewood, twenty miles away, in a light wagon, Mrs. Fowler, her boy, Artie (eight or nine years old), a yearling boy in her arms, Mother and I. After going six or eight miles, a trace came unhooked and the team stopped. Mother afterwards blamed herself for not noticing the unhooked trace and telling the team to go on. They did not go and she touched them with the whip, then too late saw the loose trace. The tongue came down. The team ran, but before the end of the tongue stuck in the ground, Mother and Mrs. Fowler were on the floor with their knees against the front endgate, each pulling a line.

The rough ride awoke us boys, asleep in the back of the wagon, and with much difficulty I made my way forward, and asked Mother not to drive so fast. About that time the tongue caught in the ground, and we went high in the air, as the wagon turned a somersault. Perhaps we were all knocked out for a short time. I arose from the ground with my nose bleeding copiously, saw Artie already up, and saw my mother arise and look around until she spotted the team, far away and running hard toward home, but Mrs. Fowler and the baby were nowhere to be seen. Mother went to the over-turned wagon box and lifted up one end. Mrs. Fowler crawled out from underneath with the babe on her arm.

This happened near the Riggs homestead and very soon Mr. Riggs and his son were out to help us to their house.

They caught the team and I think they must have taken us and the team back home, neither Mrs. Fowler, Mother nor the wagon being fit for further travel at that time. Mother and Mrs. Fowler had badly-bruised knees and sore arms, Artie had a scratch on his hand, I, my nosebleed, but the baby was unscathed. How lucky we were!

At the time of the "Indian scare", when the Sioux Indians left the reservation and refused to return, and the soldiers were sent to bring them back, there was much apprehension among the scattered settlers out away from the Black Hills and all manner of rumors were rife. One was that the Indians and soldiers had met, with the soldiers wiped out, with the settlers wiped out, and the Indians coming our way. A twelve-year-old girl, living alone with her mother about a mile-and-a-half farther out than we, rode through the night telling people to fly, the Indians were coming. Her mother had a flair for dramatics.

We did not fly, not right then, but Father kept the team in the barn harnessed night and day, and finally he hitched them up and sent Mother and Joe and me to Whitewood. Just two days was enough for Mother, and then she took us back home. I don't think Father was really pleased to see us but made the best of it. The government had issued rifles to the settlers and quite a number, we among them, established themselves at Vale, turning it into sort of an armed camp. Eventually word came that all was safe, but I remember the old army rifle standing behind the kitchen door for months after that.

Mother had an important part in organizing and maintaining and operating a Sunday School which was well-attended for a number of years in the little rural school house a mile or so from our home.

Father and Mother met every hardship and setback with courage and fortitude, and always had soft and loving hands for our aches and ailments. People had little severe illness, babies came into the world without the service of a doctor, and the very few people that returned to earth had the services of a minister but not that of an undertaker.228

Ella Grant Ames Vallery
Butte County
1883

    Ella Grant graduated from the Mankato (Minnesota) Normal School in 1877, then taught in the Worthington public schools until she was married to George R. Ames in 1879. In 1881, Mr. Ames passed away, leaving his widow with two small sons.
    In 1883, Judge H.J. Grant (Mrs. Ames' father) trailed sheep -- the first to come to this area -- from New Mexico, to a place on the Belle Fourche river about twelve miles east of Belle Fourche. Mr. Grant had expected to make a home for himself and daughter and sons in Deadwood, but finding no empty houses there to live in, moved on down to the Belle Fourche river where he was grazing his sheep.
    He wished to establish a home here and arranged for his daughter to live with him. And there the home was established, a dugout made on the south side of the Belle Fourche river in a high bank overlooking the river bottom on which was a grove of cottonwood trees, about twelve miles below the present site of Belle Fourche. Mrs. Ames papered the dugout with newspapers, and furnished it attractively with cupboards and book shelves (many of them homemade). Her library, containing the largest number of books of any home in the community at that time, attracted many visitors. She partitioned her home into three rooms with carpets.
    The dugout was clean, neat and cozy, with that invisible atmosphere which makes a real home, and in which Mr. Grant, Mrs. Ames and her sons began their South Dakota life.
    The front door of the dugout, to the north, opened on a beautiful view of a river bottom, grassy, with large cottonwood trees making lovely, shady places for outdoor meals and picnics. A winding path with flatrock steps led down the hill to a spring of water -- crystal clear. Judge Grant had used his homestead right in Minnesota so Mrs. Ames filed on the land as a homestead.
    The Beam schoolhouse, now known as Hillside, was built soon after Mrs. Ames located in her dugout home, and she was asked to teach. The following year she was placed on the "Cowboy" political ticket as a candidate for the first Butte County

superintendent of schools, serving in this capacity from 1884 until 1891. Butte county had separated from Lawrence, and then included what is now Butte, Harding and Perkins counties. She received a salary of $100.00 per year plus $2.50 per each school visited.229

Visiting country schools, Mrs. Ames traveled over the prairies in a buckboard, taking her two small sons with her. There were no highways, roads were merely trails across the prairie. Sometimes, going to schools not too great distance, she rode horseback, on a side saddle.

Looking backward, Mrs. Vallery says: "But those were happy days. People were kind, good neighbors, and enjoyed themselves. One of the principal amusements were the dances held usually in the kitchen because that was the largest room in most of the houses. They called them the 'kitchen sweats'".

There were no doctors in the neighborhood and Mrs. Ames had a large doctor book, armed with which she visited the sick.

At one time, when holding a teacher's institute in Minnesela, Mrs. Ames had the pleasure of meeting and talking with Susan B. Anthony and Anna Shaw who were on a lecture tour through the west.*

While county superintendent, she held at one time in Minnesela an "Afternoon With Authors." She has a letter written her by John G. Whittier replying to her request for something of his life not published.

Mrs. Ames was united in marriage with P. P. Vallery, farmer and rancher of the neighborhood, in 1892. Member of many clubs, she was always interested in, and working for, improvement in the community. Probably the first club ever organized in the county was a girl's club which she organized with the older girls of the school, the D.U.O., on the principle of the Golden Rule. In 1940, she was elected by South Dakota State College as Eminent Homemaker of western South Dakota. Her picture hangs in the hall of fame at the college. 230

Lucy Volland
Meade County
[1882]

"When I graduated from driving a team of oxen to driving a team of horses, I thought I was somebody," said Lucy Volland of Lead.

When only six years old, she came with her parents into the West. The covered wagon in which they made the journey was crowded as there were nine children, one an adopted child. The wagon was drawn by oxen and behind it, twenty-five head of cattle drifted along while the barefooted children took turns in keeping the cattle moving. Like Annie Tallent, Lucy walked part of the way into the Hills without shoes, although she had a pair of "plow shoes", as they called the heavy shoes in use at that time.

"We would stop and make camp at night and at one farm near Salem, the people were using twisted hay for fuel. It was slew grass and they twisted it into a figure eight, the right length for the cook stove.

"There were numerous herd of buffalo along the way and it made the meat problem simple for mother. My brother would ask what kind of meat she wanted, then go shoot either a buffalo, deer, or antelope," recalls Lucy.

Once when her brother was "cutting up a critter" an Indian came along and took possession of the insides of the animal. What he wanted with it was anybody's guess.*

Those early pioneers who braved all kinds of perils and hardships to settle this country were good at make-shift. When Lucy's mother ran out of coffee she scooped up some dried peas and browned them for coffee, and it "tasted pretty good." At night the family would grind the corn for their breakfast hotcakes.

They settled near Sturgis where her father took a homestead. "Like lots of pioneer families we lived in a tent for a time and I see no cause to be ashamed of it," remarked Lucy. "We managed all right in the tent until Father could stick up a frame house. Everybody worked hard and I recall that father sometimes sowed as high as a hundred acres of wheat by hand and that was hard work, walking so much to scatter the grain. My sister and I used to cut up the corn by hand for the stock."

Their nearest neighbor was two miles away, which was quite close for South Dakota in those days. Rattlesnakes were numerous and the Keffler children were paid a bounty of five cents a head for helping rout the snakes by killing them.

"I never got to go to school but nine days in my whole life. I always had to do a man's work, but I guess it didn't hurt me, though. There was no school close enough and no post office at first as we lived eighteen miles from Sturgis. Maybe that doesn't sound far these days, but with a team of oxen hitched to the big wagon it seemed to take my father forever to make the trip there and back."

"When I was about ten-years-old, I got out and plowed for my father and I must have been a pretty fair bullwhacker to manage those oxen that well. When father got horses for me to plow with, that was an event. I used to whoop and sing to attract folks passing and I'd call out, 'look, we got horses!'"

The Kefflers were afraid of Indians, so Keffler dug back into the hill beside the house and made a large circular underground room. They had to crawl in on their hands and knees, but it served the need. One Indian scare proved a false alarm and about all it did was to furnish neighbors an excuse to come for a visit because of the shelter.

"I recall that two white men killed a very old man and burned down his shack. The two men broke jail, but law officers brought out a troop of soldiers and between them and the settlers they caught the two criminals."

"This may sound odd now, but I did not even get in to see the town of Sturgis until I was eighteen-years-old. Then the excitement of seeing so many houses and people all at once made me sick ... nerves, I guess you would call it now."

Lucy was rummaging around and soon brought out a dog-eared tablet which explains why she uses good language. In the tablet she would carefully put down new words as she would hear them, so she could learn to use them. In this way she has steadily added new words to her vocabulary.

Her self-education has come the hard way, and much of it acquired since she was grown. Her father proved up on the land and moved into Sturgis but by that time she was grown and did not take to the idea of going in with the little children to school. Many a child had to forego education in those early days and it was not due to the indifference of parents, either.

She lived two doors from Annie Tallent and knew her and her son, Bob, very well.

Once they got settled in Sturgis there were no fields for Lucy to plow nor rattlers strolling around waiting to be killed at five cents each, so Lucy got a job in the Fruth Hotel.

For $1.00 a day she baked buns, scrubbed her half of the kitchen floor and laundered the large tablecloths. Her shift was a ten hour deal, and except for some clothes money, she gave her folks every cent.

"A dollar a day wasn't bad then. We could buy a pound of butter and a pound of coffee and have change left, and now look at prices. We used to get ten cents a dozen for eggs and we raised our own food when we lived on the farm."

She recalls the terrible blizzards while on the farm. "At times the snow would get so deep the men had to go out of the second-story window, walking on the crusted, hard snow to get to the barn. They would tie ropes around their waists so they could find the way back."

The young lady met and fell in love with a young grocery clerk named Bob Volland and the two were married. For two years they lived in Sturgis, then moved to Lead.

When the young bride first saw Lead there were many logs lying around on Main Street. The town was small and the main street ran all the way down the hill. At that time, Lead had two depots.

For years her husband worked in the Hearst store, and for a year-and-a-half operated the Alva, Wyoming, store for the Homestake. When that store was closed he returned to his old job in Lead.

The Vollands had no children of their own, so one day, when someone told Lucy about a "cute baby" at the Sister's School, she told her husband in a joke that she was going to adopt her. A few days later he said, "I thought you said we'd adopt that kid," then he added, "go get her" and that was exactly what they did. The baby had been deserted, and they never knew who her people were nor how old she was. She seemed about a year old at the time, so the Vollands settled for that. The child had no clothes so they threw a coat around her and headed for their home. "That adopted daughter we soon learned to love as our own," said Lucy.231

1. Mrs. Price, 1949, p. 8-9, MSS. (Poem written by her sister). Alice Hough Price, Meade County, 1882. PDC.
2. Laura Russell Sentman, "History of Thomas H. Russell Family," MSS. Laura Russell Sentman, Lawrence County, 1878. PDC.
3. Lois Miller, "Injured Spearfish Lady, 89, Undaunted," Rapid City Journal, n.d. Laura Wilson, Lawrence County, 1904. PDC.
4. MSS. May Holcomb White, Pennington County, 1879. PDC.
5. Martha Lewis Hughes, Pennington County, 1877. PDC.
6. Thomas Odell, "Historic Hills Incidents Recalled by Widow of Rapid City's Founder," unidentified newspaper clipping, n.d. Mrs. Samuel F. Scott, Pennington County, 1877. PDC.
7. Mrs. Parker, "Pioneer Days in the Black Hills," 1950, MSS. Emma Parker, Lawrence County, 1877. PDC.
8. Anna Wood Berryman, Meade County, 1880. PDC.
9. Mrs. C. A. Syverson, MSS. Anna Simm Brooks, Lawrence County, 1884. PDC.
10. Lois Miller, "Pioneer Central City Pair Recalls Mine Booms, Strike," Rapid City Journal, 22 November 1953, p. 12. Nettie Tuller Blow, Lawrence County, 1877. PDC.
11. Margaret Lillian Hunter Howe, Lawrence County, 1879. PDC.
12. Ruby M. Lee, "Hills Termed Wild, Lawless Says Pioneer," Rapid City, South Dakota, Daily Journal, 28 July 1953, p, 6. Mrs. Maurice Holly, Pennington County, 1890. PDC.
13. Lois Miller, "Hot Springs' 'First Lady' Recalls Vigilante Threat," Rapid City Journal, 2 May 1954. Mattie Dennis Turner, Fall River County, 1878. PDC.
14. Edith Cole, "Lone Survivor Tells of Adventurous Trek," unidentified newspaper clipping, n.d. Anna Lambert, Fall River County, 1881. PDC.
15. Lois Miller, "Custer Woman's Home Way Station For School Kids," Rapid City, South Dakota, Daily Journal, 13 February 1955, p. 14. Mrs. Gus Carlson, Custer County, 1889. PDC.
16. Margaret Martin, MSS. Triphena Campion Littlefield Johnson, Butte County, [latter part of 1890's]. PDC.
17. Marie Thybo Sorensen, "Dakota Pioneer Corsage," MSS. Christena Callesen, Yankton County, 1880. PDC.

18. "Pioneer Profile," Rapid City Journal, 12 March 1950. Nancy Woods, Butte County, [before 1889]. PDC.
19. Jean Hill & Mary L. Aschenbrenner from information provided by Madison Ballantyne, Mrs. Ballantyne's son, "Martha Ballantyne," Lead Junior Nugget, 16 November 1951, p. 16 & 36. Martha Alice Moralee Ballantyne, Lawrence County, 1879. PDC.
20. Hannah Elward, MSS. Ethelreda Browning Wringrose, Lawrence County, 1878. PDC.
21. Hannah Elward, September 1957, MSS. Mabel Grace Cachelin Wolfe, Lawrence County, 1881. PDC.
22. "Mrs. Thompson Dies Monday in Spearfish," unidentified newspaper clipping, 11 August 1953, p. 3. Carolyn Thompson, Lawrence County, 1879. PDC.
23. Myrtle Danks (daughter), MSS. Andy Ball Family, Fall River County, 1885. PDC.
24. Jettie A. McCracken Magnet, Lawrence County, 1880. PDC.
25. Mrs. Ralph Gordon, MSS, 1954. Rebecca Ann Thomas Payton Doud, Pennington County, 1880. PDC.
26. Jim Dash, MSS. Orpha LeGros Haxby, Pennington County, 1876. PDC.
27. Helena Kresse Lampert, Pennington County, 1881. PDC.
28. Margaret Martin, MSS. Jennie Wells Hubbard, Lawrence County, 1882. PDC.
29. Elizabeth A. Hunter, Lawrence County, 1879. PDC.
30. Warren Morrell, "Thru the Hills," unidentified newspaper clipping, n.d. Minnie Massey, Lawrence County, 1877. PDC.
31. Marna Velzy, "The Journey to a New Home," Lead Junior Nugget, 16 November 1951, p. 57. Susie Lane Wagner, Lawrence County, 1879. PDC.
32. Louise G. Curran, 1954, MSS. Emma Almire Vickers, Lawrence County, 1880. PDC.
33. Mrs. Robert Koontz, MSS. Rebecca Weber, Lawrence County, 1885. PDC.
34. Andrew E. Anderson to Mrs. W. E. Rodeniser, MSS. Elna Johnson Anderson, Meade County, 1879. PDC.
35. Hannah Elward, MSS. Mary Hessinger Rickel, Lawrence County, 1877. PDC.

36. Mrs. D. B. Hilton, "Pioneer Profile," unidentified newspaper clipping, n.d. Mrs. G.W. Mossing, Lawrence County, 1880. PDC.
37. Lois Miller, "Lead Woman Can Remember Early Hills Life, '79 Fire," Lead Daily Call, 16 July 1956, p. 2.; Marna Velzy, "Mae Stilwell Berry," Lead Junior Nugget, 16 November 1951, p. 18. May Stillwell Berry, Lawrence County, 1880. PDC.
38. Mrs. Marion Lutey, MSS, "Biography of Jessie May Huff 'Schultz-Conners'", 1958. Jessie May Huff Connors, Lawrence County, 1877. PDC.
39. Mrs. George Baggaley, MSS. Jennie Evans Baggaley, Lawrence County, 1877. PDC.
40. Mrs. Clark, MSS, 1949. Kate Pohlzon Clark, Pennington County, 1885. PDC.
41. Mildred Fielder, MSS. Annie Bratfoss Johnson, Lawrence County, 1878. PDC.
42. Mrs. Granville Rockefeller, Lawrence County, 1877. PDC.
43. "Mrs. Belle Parker to Observe 75th Year in Deadwood on February 22," unidentified newspaper clipping, 22 February 1951. Belle Parker, Lawrence County, 1876. PDC.
44. A. Belle Riley, "Old Time Resident of Deadwood Leaves for California," Lead Junior Nugget, 16 November 1951. Belle Parker, Lawrence County, 1876. PDC.
45. "Beulah Madsen Hansen," MSS. Beulah Madsen Hansen, Pennington County, 1910. PDC.
46. Cora Allen Headding, Aurora County, 1876. PDC.
47. Lois Miller, "Injured Spearfish Lady, 89, Undaunted," Rapid City Journal, n.d. Laura Wilson, Lawrence County, 1904. PDC.
48. Mrs. Wm. Lutey and Mrs. M. O'Brien, MSS. Laura Ann Kinchelo Dickinson, Lawrence County, 1883. PDC.
49. Lois Miller, "Deadwood Lady, 85, Prefers Hills Home," Rapid City Journal, n.d. Theresa Geis Ashe, Lawrence County, 1879. PDC.
50. Mrs. O.B. Williams, Fall River County, 1890. PDC.
51. Mrs. A.C. Boland, Pennington County, 1878. PDC.
52. Victoria Pioney Murphy, Pennington County, 1888. PDC.
53. Mrs. O.B. Williams, Fall River County, 1890. PDC.
54. Josephine B. Richards, MSS; Olive Railsback Brown, Meade County, 1880. PDC.
55. Clara Kuntz Jarvis, Meade County, 1882, PDC.

56. Mrs. Winnie J. Tubbs, MSS, March 1951. Hila Freeman Wallace, Fall River County, 1887. PDC.
57. MSS. Helene C. Pohlzon, Pennington County, 1885. PDC.
58. Lois Miller, "Hill City Pioneer Recalls Early Days in Heart O'Hills," Rapid City Journal, n.d. Mrs. Ben Mills, Pennington County, [188?]. PDC.
59. Lois Miller, "Pioneer Sturgis Merchant Slept With Six Guns," Rapid City Journal, n.d. Inga Nordgren Anderson, Lawrence and Meade Counties, 1877. PDC.
60. Mrs. Winnie J. Tubbs, MSS, March 1951. Hila Freeman Wallace, Fall River County, 1887. PDC.
61. Edith Cole, "Lone Survivor Tells of Adventurous Trek," unidentified newspaper clipping, n.d. Anna Lambert, Fall River County, 1881. PDC.
62. Lois Miller, "Sundance Pioneer Has Had Full Life In West River," Rapid City, South Dakota, Daily Journal, 25 September 1955, p. 2. Ada A. Ernest, Butte County, 1890. PDC.
63. Lois Miller, "Widow of Civil War Vet Recalls Housekeeping Hazards on Prairie," Rapid City Journal, 9 November 1952, p.
64. Margaret Martin, MSS. Eleanor Castleman Small, Butte County, 1894. PDC.
65. MSS. Josephine Akey Gushurst, Lawrence County, 1878. PDC.
66. Lois Miller, "Custer Woman's Home Way Station For School Kids," Rapid City, South Dakota, Daily Journal, 13 February 1955, p. 14. Mrs. Gus Carlson, Custer County, 1889. PDC.
67. Copied by Margaret Martin, MSS. Lucinda Davis, Butte County, 1878. PDC.
68. Jean Hill & Mary L. Aschenbrenner from information provided by Madison Ballantyne, Mrs. Ballantyne's son, "Martha Ballantyne," Lead Junior Nugget, 16 November 1951, p. 16 & 36. Martha Alice Moralee Ballantyne, Lawrence County, 1879. PDC.
69. "Nisland Pair Has Recollections of Pioneer Hardship," Rapid City, South Dakota, Daily Journal, 4 April 1957, p. 6, Mary Ann Mayer Comes, Hutchinson County, 1884. PDC.
70. Mrs. George Baggaley, MSS. Jennie Evans Baggaley, Lawrence County, 1877. PDC.
71. Florence Hett, "A Pioneer of South Dakota: Hilda Hett," MSS. Hilda Hett, Lawrence and Harding Counties, 1885. PDC

72. Mildred Fielder, MSS. Jennie Neal Boylan, Lawrence County, 1876. PDC.
73. Mrs. Willard H. Warren, MSS. Agnes Ann Campion, Butte County, 1897. PDC.
74. Hester Ensor Kuenster, Pennington County, 1885. PDC.
75. Annie Winfield Hough, Lawrence County, 1882. PDC.
76. Myrtle Danks (daughter), MSS. Andy Ball Family, Fall River County, 1885. PDC.
77. Warren Morrell, "Thru the Hills," unidentified newspaper clipping, n.d. Odena Rail, Lawrence County, 1882. PDC.
78. "First Couple Married in Lead Celebrate 73rd Year Together," unidentified newspaper clipping, n.d. Josephine Akey Gushurst, Lawrence County, 1878. PDC.
79. MSS. May Holcomb White, Pennington County, 1879. PDC.
80. Mrs. Price, 1949, p. 4-5, MSS. Alice Hough Price, Meade County, 1882. PDC.
81. Hannah Elward, September 1957, MSS. Mabel Grace Cachelin Wolfe, Lawrence County, 1881. PDC.
82. MSS. Sophronia Fell Monismith Gorum, Lawrence County, 1882. PDC.
83. Warren Morrell, "Thru the Hills," unidentified newspaper clipping, n.d. Odena Rail, Lawrence County, 1882. PDC.
84. Lois Miller, "Deadwood Lady, 85, Prefers Hills Home," Rapid City Journal, n.d. Theresa Geis Ashe, Lawrence County, 1879. PDC.
85. Synome Termes and Phyllis Krause, "Interview of Mrs. Wright," Lead Junior Nugget, 16 November 1951, p. 24, Angie Wright, Lawrence County, 1890. PDC.
86. Lois Miller, "Hill City Pioneer Recalls Early Days in Heart O'Hills," Rapid City Journal, n.d. Mrs. Ben Mills, Pennington County, [188?]. PDC.
87. Mrs. Anna Wood Berryman, Meade County, 1880. PDC.
88. Lois Miller, "Pioneer Sturgis Merchant Slept With Six Guns," Rapid City Journal, n.d. Inga Nordgren Anderson, Lawrence and Meade Counties, 1877. PDC.
89. Lois Miller, "Old-Timer Recalls Deadwood's Heyday, Rapid City Journal, n.d. Mrs. Ole Peterson, Lawrence County, 1892. PDC.

90. Thomas Odell, "Historic Hills Incidents Recalled by Widow of Rapid City's Founder," unidentified newspaper clipping, n.d. Mrs. Samuel F. Scott, Pennington County, 1877. PDC.
91. Mrs. Charles Ewing, MSS, 1954. Libbie Ann Boland Harter, Pennington County, 1879. PDC.
92. Mrs. Anna Wood Berryman, Meade County, 1880. PDC.
93. Helen Otto, "Pioneer Profile." unident. news., n.d. Barbara G. K. Mahnken, Lawrence County, 1878.
94. Jean Hill & Mary L. Aschenbrenner from information provided by Madison Ballantyne, Mrs. Ballantyne's son, "Martha Ballantyne," Lead Junior Nugget, 16 November 1951, p. 16 & 36. Martha Alice Moralee Ballantyne, Lawrence County, 1879. PDC.
95. Lois Miller, "Hill City Pioneer Recalls Early Days in Heart O'Hills," Rapid City Journal, n.d. Mrs. Ben Mills, Pennington County, 188?, PDC.
96. Amanda Oyler, "Black Hills Pioneers Provided Own Amusements, Had Good Time," unidentified newspaper clipping, n.d. Mrs. Ada Nelson, Lawrence County, 1877. PDC.
97. Lois Miller, "Old-Timer Recalls Deadwood's Heyday, Rapid City Journal, n.d. Mrs. Ole Peterson, Lawrence County, 1892. PDC.
98. Lois Miller, "Injured Spearfish Lady, 89, Undaunted," Rapid City Journal, n.d. Laura Wilson, Lawrence County, 1904. PDC.
99. Thomas Odell, "Historic Hills Incidents Recalled by Widow of Rapid City's Founder," unidentified newspaper clipping, n.d. Mrs. Samuel F. Scott, Pennington County, 1877. PDC.
100. Mrs. Charles Ewing, MSS, 1954. Libbie Ann Boland Harter, Pennington County, 1879. PDC.
101. Mrs. Parker, "Pioneer Days in the Black Hills," 1950, MSS. Emma Parker, Lawrence County, 1877. PDC.
102. Amanda Oyler, "Black Hills Pioneers Provided Own Amusements, Had Good Time," unidentified newspaper clipping, n.d. Ada Nelson, Lawrence County, 1877. PDC.
103. Lois Miller, "Nonagenarian Recalls Homesteading Trials," Rapid City Journal, n.d. Susan Morehouse, Meade County, 1888. PDC.
104. Lucy A. Trent, Fall River County, 1898. PDC.

105. Joe Carr, "Lottie Emery," Lead Junior Nugget, 16 November 1951, p. 28. Lottie Emery, Lawrence County, 1900. PDC.
106. Lois Miller, "Widow of Civil War Vet Recalls Housekeeping Hazards on Prairie," Rapid City Journal, 9 November 1952, p. 5. Margaret A. Carter, Meade County, 1900. PDC.
107. Lois Miller, "Custer Woman's Home Way Station For School Kids," Rapid City, South Dakota, Daily Journal, 13 February 1955, p. 14. Mrs. Gus Carlson, Custer County, 1889. PDC.
108. Marie Thybo Sorensen, "Dakota Pioneer Corsage," MSS. Christena Callesen, Yankton County. 1880.
109. "Pioneer Profile," Rapid City Journal, 12 March 1950. Mrs. Nancy Woods, Butte County, [before 1889]. PDC.
110. Copied by Margaret Martin, MSS. Lucinda Davis, Butte County, 1878. PDC.
111. "Nisland Pair Has Recollections of Pioneer Hardship," Rapid City, South Dakota, Daily Journal, 4 April 1957, p. 6, Mary Ann Mayer Comes, Hutchinson County, 1884. PDC.
112. Marie Thybo Sorensen, "Pioneer Profiles," Belle Fourche Bee, 23 August 1951. Nellie Ashton Jenks, Butte County, 1880. PDC.
113. Hannah Elward, September 1957, MSS. Mabel Grace Cachelin Wolfe, Lawrence County, 1881. PDC.
114. Nancy Woods, Butte County, [before 1889]. PDC.
115. Lois Miller, "Injured Spearfish Lady, 89, Undaunted," Rapid City Journal, n.d. Laura Wilson, Lawrence County, 1904. PDC.
116. Ruby M. Lee, "Hills Termed Wild, Lawless Says Pioneer," Rapid City, South Dakota, Daily Journal, 28 July 1953, p, 6. Mrs. Maurice Holly, Pennington County, 1890. PDC.
117. Mrs. C. A. Syverson, MSS. Anna Simm Brooks, Lawrence County, 1884. PDC.
118. Mrs. Willard H. Warren, MSS. Agnes Ann Campion, Butte County, 1897. PDC.
119. Mrs. Willard H. Warren, MSS. Agnes Ann Campion, Butte County, 1897. PDC.
120. MSS. May Holcomb White, Pennington County, 1879. PDC.
121. Mrs. Charles Ewing, MSS, 1954. Libbie Ann Boland Harter, Pennington County, 1879. PDC.

122. Mary Jane Hocloker Judson, Meade County, 1884. PDC.
123. Ruby M. Lee, "Hills Termed Wild, Lawless Says Pioneer," Rapid City, South Dakota, Daily Journal, 28 July 1953, p, 6. Mrs. Maurice Holly, Pennington County, 1890. PDC.
124. Mrs. Ralph Gordon, MSS, 1954. Rebecca Ann Thomas Payton Doud, Pennington County, 1880. PDC.
125. Helen Otto, "Pioneer Profile." unident. news., n.d. Barbara G. K. Mahnken, Lawrence County, 1878.
126. Inez Robertson Svendby, daughter, MSS, 5 April 1956. Rose Lutz Robertson, Lawrence County, 1883; Perkins County (now Butte County), 1897. PDC.
127. Mrs. C. A. Syverson, MSS. Anna Simm Brooks, Lawrence County, 1884. PDC.
128. Lucy Peterson, "Long-Time Belle Resident Approaches Century Mark," unidentified newspaper clipping, n.d., p. 8. Sarah Brown, Butte County, 1882. PDC.
129. Myrtle Danks (daughter), MSS. Andy Ball Family, Fall River County, 1885. PDC.
130. Marie Thybo Sorensen, "Pioneer Profiles," Belle Fourche Bee, 23 August 1951. Nellie Ashton Jenks, Butte County, 1880. PDC.
131. Mary Jane Hocloker Judson, Meade County, 1868. PDC.
132. Warren Morrell, "Thru the Hills." Mary L. Tarrant, Meade County, [1895]. PDC.
133. Lois Miller, "Sundance Pioneer Has Had Full Life In West River," Rapid City, South Dakota, Daily Journal, 25 September 1955, p. 2. Ada A. Ernest, Butte County, 1890. PDC.
134. Florence Beardshear Olsen, MSS. Ella Nora Jane Van Dorn Beardshear, Pennington County, 1886. PDC.
135. MSS. Mrs. Frank Himebaugh, Pennington County, [before 1889]. PDC.
136. "Pioneer Profile," Rapid City Journal, 12 March 1950. Nancy Woods, Butte County, [before 1889]. PDC.
137. Della Westover, Custer County, 1884. PDC.
138. Ruby Lee, "Pioneer Minimizes Noted Indian Scare," Rapid City, South Dakota, Daily Journal, 8 November 1953, p. 14. Catherine Gray, Pennington County, 1886. PDC.
139. Helen Cox Odle, MSS, 1949. Mrs. James B. Cox, Meade County, 1888. PDC.

140 . Ann Aurilla MacDaniels Johnson, Custer County, 1883. PDC.
141 . Lois Miller, "Nonagenarian Recalls First Train in Hills," Rapid City Journal, 25 November 1951, p. 8. Kate Johnson Boland, Custer County, 1880. PDC.
142 . Hilda A. Muhm Crow, MSS. Hilda A. Muhm Crow, Fall River County, 1908. PDC.
143 . Jean Hill & Mary L. Aschenbrenner from information provided by Madison Ballantyne, Mrs. Ballantyne's son, "Martha Ballantyne," Lead Junior Nugget, 16 November 1951, p. 16 & 36. Martha Alice Moralee Ballantyne, Lawrence County, 1879. PDC.
144 . Copied by Margaret Martin, MSS. Lucinda Davis, Butte County, 1878. PDC.
145 . "Nisland Pair Has Recollections of Pioneer Hardship," Rapid City, South Dakota, Daily Journal, 4 April 1957, p. 6, Mary Ann Mayer Comes, Hutchinson County, 1884. PDC.
* The credulity of pioneers often knew no bounds when it came to accepting Indian stereotypes.
146 . Lois Miller, "Indian Attack Halted Literally by 'A Hair'," Rapid City Journal, n.d. Annie Cruikshank, Lawrence County, 1882. PDC.
147 . "History of Mrs. Della Zentz Kivcheloe," MSS. Della Hough Zentz Kivcheloe, Meade County, 1878. PDC.
148 . Mrs. Thomas R. Stone, MSS. I Zora Petty Francis, Fall River County, 1890. PDC.
149 . Inez Robertson Svendby, daughter, MSS, 5 April 1956. Rose Lutz Robertson, Lawrence County, 1883; Perkins County (now Butte County), 1897. PDC.
150 . "Pioneer Daughters Relate Historic Deadwood Tales," Rapid City Journal, 1 December 1953, p. 6. Maude D. Ogden, Lawrence County, 1877. PDC.
151 . Lois Miller, "Nonagenarian Recalls First Train in Hills," Rapid City Journal, 25 November 1951, p. 8. Kate Johnson Boland, Custer County, 1880. PDC.
152 . Hilda A. Muhm Crow, MSS. Hilda A. Muhm Crow, Fall River County, 1908. PDC.
153 . Lois Miller, "Widow of Civil War Vet Recalls Housekeeping Hazards on Prairie," Rapid City Journal, 9 November 1952.

154 . Jean Hill & Mary L. Aschenbrenner from information provided by Madison Ballantyne, Mrs. Ballantyne's son, "Martha Ballantyne," Lead Junior Nugget, 16 November 1951, p. 16 & 36. Martha Alice Moralee Ballantyne, Lawrence County, 1879. PDC.
155 . Mrs. Price, 1949, p. 4, MSS. Alice Hough Price, Meade County, 1882. PDC.
156 . Marie Thybo Sorensen, "Pioneer Profiles," Belle Fourche Bee, 23 August 1951. Nellie Ashton Jenks, Butte County, 1880. PDC.
157 . Florence Hett, "A Pioneer of South Dakota: Hilda Hett," MSS. Hilda Hett, Lawrence and Harding Counties, 1885. PDC.
158 . Helen Cox Odle, MSS, 1949. Mrs. James B. Cox, Meade County, 1888. PDC.
159 . Mrs. C. A. Syverson, MSS. Anna Simm Brooks, Lawrence County, 1884. PDC.
160 . Kathryn Ayer Ewing, MSS, 1954. Lillian Clark Ayer, Lawrence County, 1878. PDC.
161 . MSS. Mrs. Frank Himebaugh, Pennington County, [before 1889]. PDC.
162 . MSS. Mrs. Frank Himebaugh, Pennington County, [before 1889]. PDC.
163 . Florence Beardshear Olsen, MSS. Ella Nora Jane Van Dorn Beardshear, Pennington County, 1886. PDC.
164 . Florence Beardshear Olsen, MSS. Ella Nora Jane Van Dorn Beardshear, Pennington County, 1886. PDC.
165 . Mildred Fielder, MSS. Annie Bratfoss Johnson, Lawrence County, 1878. PDC.
166 . Ena Athalia Lancaster, MSS. Martha Cassels Lancaster, Butte County, 1884. PDC.
167 . Ann Aurilla MacDaniels Johnson, Custer County, 1883. PDC.
168 . Joe Carr, "Lottie Emery," Lead Junior Nugget, 16 November 1951, p. 28. Lottie Emery, Lawrence County, 1900, PDC.
169 . Mrs. Parker, "Pioneer Days in the Black Hills," 1950, MSS. Mrs. Emma Parker, Lawrence County, 1877, PDC.
170 . Mrs. Winnie J. Tubbs, MSS, March 1951. Hila Freeman Wallace, Fall River County, 1887. PDC.

171 . Lois Miller, "Widow of Civil War Vet Recalls Housekeeping Hazards on Prairie," Rapid City Journal, 9 November 1952, p.
172 . Rebecca Mitchell, "Pioneer Days in the Tri-State," Belle Fourche Bee, n.d. Rebecca Anne Stevens Mitchell (Mrs. William) (1887) and Mrs. Catherine Stevens (1883), Butte County, PDC.
173 . Hannah Elward, MSS, February 1958. Amalia Oppenheimer Colman, Lawrence County, 1877. PDC.
174 . Lois Miller, "Widow of Civil War Vet Recalls Housekeeping Hazards on Prairie," Rapid City Journal, 9 November 1952, p.
175 . MSS. Helene C. Pohlzon, Pennington County, 1885. PDC.
176 . "Mrs. Belle Parker to Observe 75th Year in Deadwood on February 22," unidentified newspaper clipping, 22 February 1951. Belle Parker, Lawrence County, 1876. PDC.
177 . Mrs. Charles Ewing, MSS, 1954. Libbie Ann Boland Harter, Pennington County, 1879. PDC.
178 . "Pioneer Daughters Relate Historic Deadwood Tales," Rapid City Journal, 1 December 1953, p. 6. Maude D. Ogden, Lawrence County, 1877. PDC.
179 . Amanda Oyler, "Black Hills Pioneers Provided Own Amusements, Had Good Time," unidentified newspaper clipping, n.d. Ada Nelson, Lawrence County, 1877. PDC.
180 . Helen Cox Odle, MSS, 1949. Mrs. James B. Cox, Meade County, 1888. PDC.
181 . Lois Miller, "Pioneer Central City Pair Recalls Mine Booms, Strike," Rapid City Journal, 22 November 1953, p. 12. Nettie Tuller Blow, Lawrence County, 1877. PDC.
182 . MSS. Sophronia Fell Monismith Gorum, Lawrence County, 1882. PDC.
183 . Edith Cole, "Lone Survivor Tells of Adventurous Trek," unidentified newspaper clipping, n.d. Anna Lambert, Fall River County, 1881. PDC.
184 . Lois Miller, "Sundance Pioneer Has Had Full Life In West River," Rapid City, South Dakota, Daily Journal, 25 September 1955, p. 2. Ada A. Ernest, Butte County, 1890. PDC.
185 . Hilda A. Muhm Crow, MSS. Hilda A. Crow, Fall River County, 1908. PDC.
186 . Copied by Margaret Martin, MSS. Lucinda Davis, Butte County, 1878. PDC.

187. Mrs. Willard H. Warren, MSS. Agnes Ann Campion, Butte County, 1897. PDC.
188. Marie Thybo Sorensen, "Dakota Pioneer Corsage," MSS. Christena Callesen, Yankton County, 1880. PDC.
189. Jean Hill & Mary L. Aschenbrenner from information provided by Madison Ballantyne, Mrs. Ballantyne's son, "Martha Ballantyne," Lead Junior Nugget, 16 November 1951, p. 16 & 36. Martha Alice Moralee Ballantyne, Lawrence County, 1879. PDC.
190. Marie Thybo Sorensen, "Pioneer Profiles," Belle Fourche Bee, 23 August 1951. Nellie Ashton Jenks, Butte County, 1880. PDC.
191. Lois Miller, "Pioneer Woman Recalls Early Events in Historic Deadwood," Rapid City Journal, n.d. Pauline Flormann Miller, Lawrence County, 1876. PDC.
192. Louise G. Curran, 1954, MSS. Emma Almire Vickers, Lawrence County, 1880. PDC.
193. Pamelia Arbuckle Sloan, MSS, 1954. Catherine Maud Boland Arbuckle, Pennington County, 1879. PDC.
194. Maude D. Ogden, Lawrence County, 1877. PDC.
195. Maude D. Ogden (Mrs. R. N.), Lawrence County, 1877, PDC.
196. Jim Dash, MSS. Orpha LeGros Haxby, Pennington County, 1876. PDC.
197. Nellie Hough Bradley, Meade County, 1882. PDC.
198. Mrs. Louise G. Curran, 1954, MSS. Mrs. Emma Almire Vickers, Lawrence County, 1880, PDC.
199. Kathryn Ayer Ewing, MSS, 1954. Lillian Clark Ayer, Lawrence County, 1878. PDC.
200. Ruby Lee, "Pioneer Minimizes Noted Indian Scare," Rapid City, South Dakota, Daily Journal, 8 November 1953, p. 14. Mrs. Catherine Gray, Pennington County. 1886. PDC
* The very specialized and trusted occupation of "amalgamator" was the person who removed the gold from the plates below the stamp mill. At one time the Homestake hired eight or nine of them.
201. Warren Morrell, "Thru the Hills," unidentified newspaper clipping, n.d. Odena Rail, Lawrence County, 1882. PDC.

202. Lois Miller, "Hot Springs' 'First Lady' Recalls Vigilante Threat," Rapid City Journal, 2 May 1954. Mattie Dennis Turner, Fall River County, 1878. PDC.
203. Lois Miller, "Custer Woman's Home Way Station For School Kids," Rapid City, South Dakota, Daily Journal, 13 February 1955, p. 14. Mrs. Gus Carlson, Custer County, 1889, PDC.
204. Hannah Elward, MSS. Lillian Hagerman Waugh, Pennington County, 1888. PDC.
205. Minnie Massey, Lawrence County, 1877. PDC.
206. Pamelia Arbuckle Sloan, MSS, 1954. Catherine Maud Boland Arbuckle, Pennington County, 1879. PDC.
207. Mary L. Walton, MSS, 1966. Ellen Boyce Bryant, Lawrence County, 1877. PDC.
* Deep cultural mistrust often caused the whites to misinterpret acts of kindness.
208. Edith Cole, "Indians Offered to Trade Blanket for Early Resident," Rapid City Daily Journal, 24 February 1952, p. 20. Armilda Matherly Gamet Cole, Lawrence County, 1878. PDC.
209. "Mrs. Annie Fish of Deadwood Dies," unidentified newspaper clipping, n.d.; Lois Miller, "Pioneer Profiles," Rapid City Journal, 10 December 1950, p. 20; Lois Miller, "6 Generations of Deadwood Family Have Lived in Hills," Rapid City Journal, 18 October 1953, p. 28; Carolyn Bird, "Mrs. Annie Rosenkranz Fish," Lead Junior Nugget, 16 November 1951, p. 42. Annie Rozenkranz Fish, Lawrence County, 1878. PDC.
210. Laura B. Gamut, as told to Rebecca Phillips, "Prairie Belle," The Dakota Farmer. Laura Belle Gamut, Fall River County, [before 1889].
* Bishop William Hobart Hare was sent to the Black Hills in 1880 to help found the Episcopal church.
211. Mattie Curtis Jennings, Lawrence County, 1876 and Custer County, 1882. PDC.
* A brand of refrigerator, used interchangeably for the word.
212. Lois Miller, "Central City Pioneer Says City Once Considered Most Promising," Rapid City Journal, n.d. Mrs. Clarabelle Liggett Pouriea, Lawrence County, 1893. PDC.
213. Edna Ford, "Mariah Jane Williams Ford, 1851-1924," MSS. Mariah Jane Williams Ford, Lawrence County, 1878. PDC.

214. MSS. Christina Anderson Frawley, Lawrence County, 1877. PDC.
215. Mrs. Parsons, MSS, 1951. Alvina Schleichardt Parsons, Lawrence County, 1889. PDC.
216. Mrs. Louis Grubl, MSS, 1955. Jessie Gannon Handlin Keene, Meade County, 1887. PDC.
217. Lois Miller, "Early Prairie Hardships Recalled by Pioneer Woman," Rapid City Journal, 4 January 1953. Della A. Michaels, Meade County, 1910. PDC.
* The massacre at Wounded Knee, where Big Foot was killed while his unarmed band was flying a white flag.
218. Minnie Petersen Meier, Fall River County, 1887. PDC.
219. Albert M. Hobbs, "Pioneer Profile," n.d.; "British Immigrant Found Good Life Here," Rapid City Journal, 18 July 1954, p. 21. Amelia J. Miller, Lawrence County, 1887. PDC.
220. Mary L. Mochon, "Happy Memories," 1949, MSS. Delia Doody and Mary Doody Mochon, Lawrence County, 1879. PDC.
* A sandstone tablet dated 1833, carrying a farewell message to the world from a party of gold seekers killed by Indians, was found at the base of Lookout Mountain near Spearfish by a stone mason named Louis Thoen in 1887. The stone tablet has come to be known as the Thoen Stone.
221. "Pioneer Profiles," February, 1950. Minerva Ellen Morris and Minnie Williamson, Lawrence County, 1883. PDC.
222. "History of Maude D. Ogden," MSS. Maude D. Ogden, Lawrence County, 1877. PDC.
223. "Pioneer Woman." May Edna Painter, Pennington County, 1881. PDC.
224. Barbara H. Erkkila, "Black Hills Pioneer Has Many Vivid Recollections," Rapid City Journal, 22 April 1956, p. 7. May Edna Painter, Pennington County, 1881. PDC. Editor's note: This story was written when Mrs. Painter visited her great-grandchildren in Gloucester, Massachusetts. It was written by Barbara H. Erkkila, feature writer for the Gloucester Daily Times and the Boston Sunday and Evening Globe, following an interview with Mrs. Painter.
225. Mrs. O. Leon Anderson, MSS. Alice Dinnis Ham, Pennington County, 1882. PDC.
226. MSS. Mae Florence Spruling Letteer Hudson, Pennington County, 1900. PDC.

227. Joseph T. Richards (son), MSS. Mrs. Ella Teed Richards, Butte County, 1880. PDC.
228. Harry D. Richards (son), MSS. Mrs. Ella Teed Richards, Butte County, 1880. PDC.
229. "Mrs. Ella Vallery, Butte Pioneer, Dies," unidentified newspaper clipping, 9 February, 1950, p. 8. Mrs. P. P. Vallery (Ella Grant Ames), Butte County, 1883, PDC.
* This would have been in the summer of 1890, when Susan B. Anthony and Anna Howard Shaw toured the Black Hills campaigning for the woman suffrage amendment, which was on the ballot that fall. It was defeated.
230. "Butte County Pioneer Lady Honored as one of State's Eminent Homemakers," Belle Fourche [Bee], n.d. "Mrs. Ella Vallery, Butte Pioneer, Dies," unidentified newspaper clipping, 9 February, 1950, p. 8. Ella Grant Ames Vallery, Butte County, 1883. PDC.
* To eat.
231. "Deadwood Celebration Constant Reminder of Pioneer's Birthday," Rapid City Daily Journal, 6 December 1953, p. 13. Lucy Volland, Meade County, [1882]. PDC.